2014 EYFS PROFILE - HANDBOOK

INCLUDING THE ASSESSMENT AND REPORTING ARRANGEMENTS

To purchase a copy please visit:

www.thenationalcurriculum.com

or scan this code to take you there:

D1395844

Contents

National curriculum assessments

Early Years Foundation Stage Profile

Handbook

About this publication

Who is it for?

Local authorities, headteachers, governing bodies and all Early Years education providers and education professionals with responsibility for assessing, reporting or moderating the EYFS Profile.

What does it cover?

- Information about why and how assessment should be carried out.
- Information about completing an EYFS Profile.
- Information about recording children's attainment.
- Information about making and moderating inclusive judgements for all children that are accurate and reliable.

Related information

Visit the Department for Education's website at www.education.gov.uk/assessment for all related information.

For more copies

Printed copies of this guidance are not available. It can be downloaded from the Department's website at www.education.gov.uk/assessment.

1. Introduction

1.1 The statutory framework for the Early Years Foundation Stage

The Early Years Foundation Stage (EYFS) is the statutory framework published in 2012 by the Department for Education that sets the standards for the development, learning and care of children from birth to five.

The Childcare Act Section 39(1)(a) 2006 stipulates that Early Years providers must ensure that their provision meets the learning and development requirements as specified in the EYFS (Learning and Development Requirements) Order 2007 (amended in 2012). The Act states that this Order can specify the arrangements which are required for assessing children for the purpose of ascertaining what they have achieved in relation to the early learning goals (ELGs).

As an executive agency of the Department, the Standards and Testing Agency (STA) is responsible for developing and delivering all statutory assessments from early years to the end of key stage 3. It will ensure that EYFS Profile outcomes are reliable as a result of robust moderation.

All English local authorities must have regard to any guidance produced by STA in exercising their function under the EYFS (Learning and Development Requirements) Order 2007, Section 4.2. The learning and development requirements are given legal force by an Order made under Section 39(1) (a) of the Childcare Act 2006. This can be viewed on the Government's legislation archive at: www.legislation.gov.uk/uksi/2007/1772/article/3/made.

1.2 The EYFS Profile

The EYFS Profile summarises and describes children's attainment at the end of the EYFS. It is based on ongoing observation and assessment in the three prime and four specific areas of learning, and the three characteristics of effective learning, set out below:

The prime areas of learning:

- communication and language
- physical development
- personal, social and emotional development

The specific areas of learning:

- literacy
- mathematics
- understanding the world
- expressive arts and design

Characteristics of effective learning:

- playing and exploring
- active learning
- creating and thinking critically

A completed EYFS Profile consists of 20 items of information: the attainment of each child assessed in relation to the 17 ELG descriptors, together with a short narrative describing the child's three characteristics of effective learning.

Assessments will be based primarily on observation of daily activities and events. Practitioners should note in particular the learning which a child demonstrates spontaneously, independently and consistently in a range of contexts. Accurate assessment will take account of a range of perspectives including those of the child, parents and other adults who have significant interactions with the child.

For each ELG, practitioners must judge whether a child is meeting the level of development expected at the end of the Reception year (expected), exceeding this level (exceeding), or not yet reaching this level (emerging).

The completed EYFS Profile must include a short commentary on each child's skills and abilities in relation to the three key characteristics of effective learning. This will support future curriculum planning and will provide the year 1 teacher with important information about each child's approach to learning.

1.3 Ongoing assessment

The government does not prescribe how ongoing assessment should be undertaken. The EYFS Profile is not intended to be used for ongoing assessment or for entry level assessment for Early Years settings or Reception classes.

1.4 Structure of this Handbook

The 'Handbook' has been developed to support practitioners in making accurate judgements about each child's attainment. It is supplemented by exemplification materials which are available on the Department's website at www.education.gov.uk/assessment. These enable the effective moderation of judgements so that EYFS Profile outcomes are accurate and consistent across all settings. This 'Handbook' is effective from September 2013, replacing all previous versions.

Sections 1–8 of this document provide advice and guidance on the various elements of EYFS Profile assessment, in particular:

- principles, purposes and processes of the EYFS Profile;
- completing the EYFS Profile;
- exemplification of the ELGs;
- documenting each child's attainment;
- inclusion;
- moderating EYFS Profile judgements; and
- quality assuring the assessments.

A range of documents and web based resources have been developed to assist practitioners in completing EYFS Profiles. These give the background to the statutory framework, and detail specific aspects of moderation, reporting to parents and data collection. All these resources are available on the Department's website at www.education.gov.uk/assessment.

The term 'parent' is used in this document as defined in section 576 of the Education Act 1996 as:

- parents of a child;
- any person who is not a parent of a child but who has parental responsibility for the child; and
- any person who has care of the child.

All references to EYFS settings include any out-of-home provider of early years provision for children from birth to five, such as childminders, local authority (LA) nurseries, nursery or early years centres, children's centres, playgroups, pre-schools, or schools in the independent, private or voluntary sector and maintained schools.

2. EYFS Profile purposes, principles and processes

2.1 Purposes and main uses of the EYFS Profile

The EYFS (Learning and Development Requirements) Order 2007 as amended by The EYFS (Learning and Development Requirements) (Amendment) Order 2012 specifies the learning and development requirements and gives legal effect to the EYFS statutory framework. The framework requires that the EYFS Profile is carried out in the final term of the year in which the child reaches age five, and no later than 30 June in that term.

The primary purpose of the EYFS Profile is to provide a reliable, valid and accurate assessment of individual children at the end of the EYFS.

The primary uses of EYFS Profile data are as follows. These have informed the development of the Profile.

- To inform parents about their child's development against the ELGs and the characteristics of their learning.
- To support a smooth transition to key stage 1 by informing the professional discussion between EYFS and key stage 1 teachers.
- To help year 1 teachers plan an effective, responsive and appropriate curriculum that will meet the needs of all children.

In addition, the Department considers that a secondary purpose of the assessment is to provide an accurate national data set relating to levels of child development at the end of the EYFS which can be used to monitor changes in levels of children's development and their readiness for the next phase of their education both nationally and locally (school-level results will not be published in the performance tables).

The EYFS Profile has been designed to be valid and reliable for these purposes.

2.2 Principles of EYFS Profile assessments

How an EYFS Profile is completed

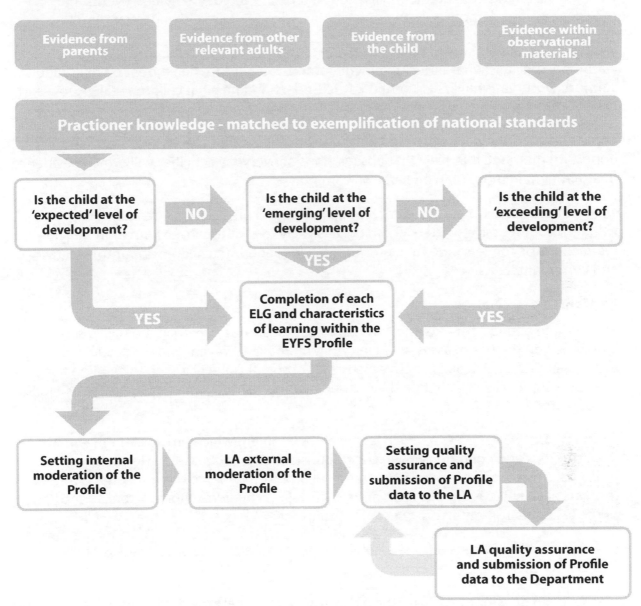

Reliable and accurate assessment at the end of the EYFS is underpinned by the following principles:

- Reliable and accurate assessment is based primarily on the practitioner's knowledge of the child gained predominantly from observation and interaction in a range of daily activities and events.
- Responsible pedagogy must be in place so that the provision enables each child to demonstrate their learning and development fully.
- Embedded learning is identified by assessing what a child can do consistently and independently in a range of everyday situations.
- An effective assessment presents a holistic view of a child's learning and development.
- Accurate assessments take account of contributions from a range of perspectives including the child, their parents and other relevant adults.

Observational assessment

Observational assessment involves reaching an understanding of children's learning by watching, listening and interacting as they engage in everyday activities, events and experiences, and demonstrate their specific knowledge, skills and understanding.

It is the most reliable way of building up an accurate picture of children's development and learning, especially where the attainment demonstrated is not dependent on overt adult support. Observational assessment is key to understanding what children really know and can do.

Some observations will be planned but some may be a spontaneous capture of an important moment. It is likely that observations of everyday activities will provide evidence of attainment in more than one area of learning.

Observational assessment does not require prolonged breaks from interaction with children, nor excessive written recording. It is likely to be interwoven with high quality interactions or conversations in words or sign language with children about their activities and current interests.

Responsible pedagogy

Responsible pedagogy enables each child to demonstrate learning in the fullest sense. It depends on the use of assessment information to plan relevant and motivating learning experiences for each child. Effective assessment can only take place when children have the opportunity to demonstrate their understanding, learning and development in a range of contexts.

Children must have access to a rich learning environment which provides them with the opportunities and conditions in which to flourish in all aspects of their development. It should provide balance across the areas of learning. Integral to this is an ethos which respects each child as an individual and which values children's efforts, interests and purposes as instrumental to successful learning.

Practitioners should consider the following when evaluating the effectiveness of their assessment processes:

- child development, both the biological and cultural aspects, and its impact on how learning may best be supported;
- planning which ensures a relevant, motivating, flexible and interesting curriculum;
- provision of an environment which truly enables successful learning by all children in their care;
- the need for detailed understanding of the framework for assessment in order to gather accurate, reliable and meaningful information;
- the importance of high quality adult interaction which is sensitive and adaptive to the needs of individual children and capable of promoting learning; and
- organisational aspects of provision, resources, curriculum and people.

The successful implementation of these aspects of pedagogy and provision provides the route from practitioner observation of individual children to an accurate, reliable and consistent assessment of their learning which will inform planning for year 1.

Child initiated activity

Key aspects of effective learning characteristics include children:

- being willing to have a go;
- being involved and concentrating;
- having their own ideas;
- choosing ways to do things;
- finding new ways; and
- enjoying achieving what they set out to do.

Accurate assessment of these characteristics depends on observing learning which children have initiated rather than only focusing on what they do when prompted. For children to develop learning characteristics to be assessed by the EYFS Profile, and to support lifelong learning, they require rich opportunities to initiate ideas and activities.

Embedded learning and secure development

A child's embedded learning and secure development are demonstrated without the need for overt adult support. Where learning is secure it is likely that children often initiate the use of that learning. Judgements about this are made through observing behaviour that a child demonstrates consistently and independently, in a range of situations. Attainment in this context will assure practitioners of the child's confidence and ownership of the specific knowledge, skill or concept being assessed. Skillful interactions with adults and learning which is supported by them are necessary on the journey to embedding skills and knowledge.

Links in the areas of learning

Areas of learning, and therefore the ELGs, are often interlinked. These in turn may be related to the characteristics of effective learning. Seeing these links will bring coherence to the assessment process and enable practitioners to capture each child's learning more effectively and genuinely. Practitioners can also reflect on these links when quality assuring their assessment judgements by examining whether the different aspects and levels of attainment make sense when considered together.

Practitioner knowledge

The majority of evidence for EYFS Profile judgements will come from the practitioner's knowledge of the child gained from observation of the child's self-initiated activities. In addition, some adult-led activities will offer insight into children's attainment, where they have the opportunity to demonstrate what they know, understand and can do.

Much evidence will be gleaned from day to day interactions with children as practitioners build up their knowledge of what children know and can do, for assessment purposes and to inform future practice and provision. This evidence, often not formally recorded, provides the basis on which judgements are made and the focus of a moderation discussion.

Contributions to the assessments

Accurate assessment will depend on contributions from a range of perspectives including the child's. Practitioners should involve children fully in their own assessment by encouraging them to communicate, and review, their own learning. The assessment should build on the insights of all adults who have significant interactions with the child. Adults with different roles will have different insights.

Accurate assessment requires a two-way flow of information between setting(s) and home. Reviews of the child's achievements should include those demonstrated at home as assessment without the parents' contribution provides an incomplete picture of a child's learning and development.

2.3 EYFS Profile assessment processes

During the final year of the EYFS, practitioners must undertake ongoing (formative) assessment to support each child's learning and development. There is no requirement that this is recorded in any specific manner or at specified points in time; practitioners should be mindful of their professional responsibility for the learning and development of every child in their care and plan the provision needed to enable children to take the next steps in their learning.

In the final term of the EYFS practitioners must review their knowledge of each child using information from all sources to make a judgement for each ELG.

 Practitioners must make a judgement for each ELG as to whether the child's learning and development is best described by:

- the description of the level of development expected at the end of the EYFS (expected);
- not yet at the level of development expected at the end of the EYFS (emerging); or
- beyond the level of development expected at the end of the EYFS (exceeding).

In making this decision, practitioners must refer to the exemplification material which is available on the Department's website at www.education.gov.uk/assessment. This material illustrates the standard expected for each ELG at the end of the EYFS.

Practitioners must consider the entirety of each ELG and avoid splitting the descriptor into sections and ticking them off when making the decision. To create the most accurate picture of the child's overall embedded learning an holistic view of the descriptor should be taken.

Judging whether a child's learning and development best fits the 'expected' category

A child's learning and development can be judged to be at the level expected at the end of the EYFS if the ELG description and accompanying exemplification best fit the practitioner's professional knowledge of the child.

Because children do not necessarily achieve uniformly, the practitioner should judge whether the description within the ELG best fits the child's learning and development, taking into account their relative strengths and weaknesses. 'Best fit' does not mean that the child has equal mastery of all aspects of the ELG. Practitioners should look to the whole of each ELG description when making this summative judgement.

If a child's learning and development does not best fit the 'expected' category

Where a child's learning and development does not yet meet what is expected at the end of the EYFS, then their learning and development is said to be at the 'emerging' level for that ELG.

Where a child's development exceeds what is expected at the end of the EYFS, attainment should be recorded within the EYFS Profile as being at the 'exceeding' level for that ELG.

To judge whether a child's learning and development is 'exceeding', practitioners should use the best fit model and be confident that the child has moved beyond the 'expected' level.

Practitioners should:

- consider the key stage 1 attainment targets and level descriptors which are available on the Department's website at www.education.gov.uk;
- refer to 'exceeding' descriptors (sourced from the Tickell review) which are provided in Annex 2 of this handbook; and
- discuss with year 1 teachers whether a child is 'exceeding' in any ELG.

Arrangements for the 'exceeding' level are interim and are subject to change once the national curriculum review is complete.

2.4 Evidence and documentation of the assessments

Practitioners should build their knowledge of what each child knows and can do over the course of the year, so that they can make an accurate end of year judgement. Settings may choose to record children's learning in any way which suits their purposes. These purposes will include supporting children's learning and development and making accurate summative assessments.

At the end of the year, practitioners must make their final EYFS Profile assessments based on all their evidence. This breadth of professional knowledge, and the exemplification of standards set out in this handbook, should be used to make judgements as to whether a child's learning meets the level expected at the end of EYFS, exceeds that level or is best described as at an 'emerging' level. Practitioners will also use the 'Handbook' when describing each child's characteristics of effective learning. These judgements are then subject to moderation in order to ensure national consistency and accuracy.

Practitioners and EYFS Profile moderators should be aware that the definition of evidence is any material, knowledge of the child, anecdotal incident or result of observation or information from additional sources that supports the overall picture of a child's development. There is no requirement that it should be formally recorded or documented; the extent to which the practitioner chooses to record information will depend on individual preference. Paperwork should be kept to the minimum that practitioners require to illustrate, support and recall their knowledge of the child's attainment.

An EYFS Profile completed by the practitioner alone will offer only a partial picture of a child's attainment. Practitioners must actively engage children, their parents and other adults who have significant interaction with the child in the assessment process.

Practitioners may include the following to support their judgements:

- knowledge of the child;
- materials which illustrate the child's learning journey, such as photographs;
- observations of day to day interactions;
- video/tape/electronic recordings;
- the child's view of his or her own learning;
- information from parents; and
- information from other relevant adults.

No assessments other than the EYFS Profile are required or expected.

2.5 Use of the EYFS Profile for transition to year 1

The transition between the EYFS and year 1 should be seamless. EYFS practitioners and year 1 teachers should work together to ensure that children's learning experiences in the final year of the EYFS are valuable in themselves, and prepare the ground for their move to year 1. It is important that year 1 builds on the successful principles and approach encapsulated in the EYFS.

It is crucial that EYFS practitioners and year 1 teachers are allocated time to discuss and expand on the information presented in the EYFS Profile. The statutory requirement at the end of EYFS is to make an accurate judgement between the three outcome bands of the EYFS profile for each of the 17 ELGs and complete the characteristics of effective learning narratives.

A principled approach to assessment ensures that a detailed holistic picture of each child's learning and development accompanies the 17 ELG decisions. The characteristic of effective learning narratives will provide significant additional detail for each child and must be included in the transition discussion.

Beyond the 20 items of the EYFS profile, practitioners may provide any additional information needed to enable year 1 teachers to plan an effective curriculum and provision for all children. Decisions about this additional information should be made by each setting and reflect the characteristics and requirements of that setting. This will enable the year 1 teacher to have a fully rounded picture of the attainment of each child in order to plan the curriculum. Year 1 teachers should be involved in EYFS Profile moderation in order for them to understand the judgements made by Early Years practitioners.

3. Inclusion

The EYFS Profile is an inclusive assessment, capable of capturing a wide range of children's learning and development outcomes. For some children, the processes of observation and assessment present a particular challenge to practitioners, which must be addressed for attainment to be accurately judged and recorded. This challenge applies both to

- understanding how some children might demonstrate attainment at the level expected at the end of the EYFS; and
- how to capture the attainment of children whose development is judged to be at the 'emerging' level.

3.1 Children with special educational needs and disability

The range of special educational needs and disability (SEND) is diverse and includes physical, emotional, sensory and learning needs.

For children with SEND the setting will develop additional relationships with other professionals. It is vital that communication between all professionals and the child's parent is strong so that a clear picture is gained of the child's learning and development.

Observational assessment is the most effective way of making judgements about all children's learning and development. Depending on their special educational need, children will demonstrate their learning and development in different ways. Practitioners observing the child involved in day to day activities must take account of the following:

- with the exception of ELG03 Speaking, where the EYFS Profile contains the word 'talks' or 'speaks' children can use their established or preferred mode of communication; and

- the need to be alert to the child demonstrating attainment in a variety of ways, including eye pointing, use of symbols or signs.

Any adaptations children use to carry out their activities, such as mobility aids, magnification or adapted ICT equipment, should be employed so that practitioners come to know all children at their most capable.

Where a child's learning and development does not yet meet the description of the level expected at the end of the EYFS for an individual ELG, the outcome will be recorded as 'emerging'. Practitioners should also record details of any specific assessment and provision in place for the child, and use this comprehensive record as a basis for discussion with parents and to support planning for future learning. This will ensure that parents have a clear, rounded picture of their child's development and are informed about additional support and future activities.

Please note that P scales are an assessment tool designed for use at key stage 1 and should not be used for assessing children in the EYFS.

3.2 Children for whom English is not their home language

The communication skills of children for whom English is not their home language are not all the same. These children will be at different stages of learning English and one or more other languages. Learning English as an additional language is not a special educational need. Practitioners need to find out as much as they can about a child's prior language experience and any education experienced elsewhere. Parents, as the first educators, are an important source of information.

Underpinning the EYFS Profile assessment is the understanding that language is central to our sense of identity and belonging to a community, and that linguistic diversity is a strength that is recognised and valued. Practitioners may need to help parents understand that a child's home language development will help them learn English.

Parents also need to know that it is perfectly acceptable, even desirable, for the child's home language to be used in the setting. Practitioners will need to observe the child over time and raise questions with the parents, and/or bilingual support assistants, to be confident about what the child knows and understands.

There are three aspects specific to the assessment of children for whom English is not their home language:

- development in their home language;
- development across areas of learning, assessed through their home language; and
- development of English.

Within the EYFS Profile, the ELGs for communication and language and for literacy must be assessed in relation to the child's competency in English. The remaining ELGs may be assessed in the context of any language – including the child's home language and English.

This has implications for provision. The principles of good practice for children learning English are the principles of good practice for all children. Children must have opportunities to engage in activities and first-hand experiences that do not depend solely on English for success, and where they can participate in ways that reveal what they know and can do in the security of their home language. For children to grow in confidence, and hence demonstrate their embedded learning, their environment must reflect their cultural and linguistic heritage and their learning be supported by a wide range of stimuli and experiences.

3.3 Children from minority groups

The ethnicities of children within a setting can be diverse, particularly in urban settings. The children may be refugees or asylum seekers, their families may have histories of persecution and trauma, or they may have had positive experiences but different cultural conventions governing behaviours and gender roles. This cultural background may also determine how early education is perceived, and how much experience of school or another Early Years setting the child may have had prior to their EYFS Profile assessment.

Children may come from settled communities or travel frequently. This latter consideration affects minority groups such as Gypsy, Roma and Traveller children as well as children with armed forces, embassy and global corporate backgrounds.

Practitioners must take particular care that the environment echoes children's own positive experiences. Children will be able to demonstrate their attainment when opportunities such as role play, cookery, celebrations and visits to special places or events are linked to their cultural experience. This will also be captured in the narrative relating to characteristics of learning, where the child's ability to begin their play and exploration with things which are familiar and build new knowledge and learning from this starting point, are expressly considered (Playing and exploring: using what they know in their play).

The relationship with parents is crucial to developing the practitioners' knowledge of the child and their ability to make an accurate assessment. Parents can help practitioners understand the different values that explain their child's responses to the environment and social situations. A child will find it easier to express their feelings and feel confident in their learning if practitioners listen and respond in ways that show understanding.

3.4 Taking account of the needs of individual children

Reaching accurate assessments using the EYFS Profile requires practitioners to enable all children to reach their full potential. Consequently, practitioners must be alert to the general diversity of children's interests, needs and inclinations.

For instance, there may be children who are at an earlier stage of development than others in the cohort; some may have summer birthdays. These children and others may be highly active and more likely to demonstrate what they know, understand and can do in situations which are sympathetic to this inclination, often outdoors.

Practitioners should reflect on their observations and ensure that the provision enables all children, regardless of their stage of development or interests, needs and inclinations, to demonstrate attainment in ways that are motivating to them.

3.5 Transition conversations for children with an outcome at the 'emerging' level

Where children have an outcome of 'emerging' for an ELG, it is likely that this will not provide full information about their learning and development at the end of the EYFS. Additional information should be considered alongside EYFS Profile outcomes, to ensure that conversations between EYFS and year 1 staff are meaningful, and lead to a successful transition for the child.

An outcome of 'emerging' may mask a wide range of levels of learning and development, the detail of which is built over time through observation, interaction with the child and ongoing assessment. There are many sources of information about how children learn and develop, how this may be manifested and how further learning and development might be supported. There is no requirement on practitioners to use any specific source of information in this context.

Specialist professional guidance is available for many specific special educational needs and disabilities. Children with SEND may have records from professionals within and outside of the setting. These records should inform the assessment and transition processes. Wherever possible other professionals working with the child should be invited to contribute to transition conversations.

The provision of additional information around the 20 items of the EYFS Profile, in order to support successful transition and a smooth learning journey for the child, should be considered by settings in advance of the summer term so that processes can be built on shared understanding, thoroughly planned, and implemented in good time. Decisions about what sources of guidance might be used and what additional information shared, should be made at a setting level and reflect local needs and circumstances.

4. Completing the EYFS Profile

Settings should refer to the 2014 EYFS 'Assessment and reporting arrangements' (ARA) for more information about current requirements. This will be available later in the autumn term.

4.1 Making EYFS Profile assessments

Assessment against the 17 ELGs and the three characteristics of effective learning must be made in the summer term of the academic year in which the child reaches age five, in accordance with the statutory framework.

Taking into account all the evidence from a range of sources, practitioners will match their view of each child's attainment to the exemplification of national standards and the guidance on characteristics of effective learning. This will lead to judgements of attainment and to the nature of each child's learning characteristics.

4.2 Recording children's attainment

Once EYFS Profile judgements have been made the practitioner should record each child's level of development against the 17 ELGs as 'emerging', 'expected' or 'exceeding'. Practitioners must complete the profile with a brief commentary on the child's skills and abilities in relation to the three key characteristics of effective learning, following the guidance in section 4.4.

A sample proforma to support recording is provided in Annex 1, although there is no requirement for settings to use this format.

4.3 Exceptions and exemptions

The EYFS Profile should be completed during the summer term of the academic year in which a child reaches age five unless:

- an exemption from the Profile has been granted for the setting or an individual child by the Secretary of State;
- the child is continuing in EYFS provision beyond the year in which they turn five;
- the child has recently arrived from abroad and so an accurate and valid assessment cannot be completed; or
- the child has spent a lengthy period of time away from the setting, for example, due to illness or medical treatment.

In these instances the practitioner should refer to the ARA for further guidance about the circumstances in which these decisions will be considered valid, and the associated requirements placed upon settings.

4.4 Characteristics of effective learning

The characteristics of effective learning describe factors which play a central role in a child's learning and in becoming an effective learner. They are vital elements of support for the transition process from EYFS to year 1. The characteristics of effective learning run through and underpin all seven areas of learning and development, representing processes rather than outcomes. Information describing the child's characteristics of effective learning will provide year 1 teachers with vital background and context when considering the child's next stage of development and future learning needs.

The commentary should consist of a short description (ie one to two paragraphs) of how the child demonstrates the three key characteristics of effective learning:

- playing and exploring;
- active learning; and
- creating and thinking critically.

These descriptions must reflect ongoing observation of the child within formative assessment processes and should take account of all relevant records held by the setting and include information from the child, their parents and other relevant adults.

The table below provides information relating to each of the characteristics of effective learning.

Please refer to Annex 3 for examples of some possible lines of enquiry when completing the commentary for each characteristic of effective learning.

Playing and exploring - engagement

Finding out and exploring is concerned with the child's open-ended hands-on experiences which result from innate curiosity and provide raw sensory material from which the child builds concepts, tests ideas and finds out.

Using what they know in their play describes how children use play to bring together their current understandings, combining, refining and exploring their ideas in imaginative ways. Representing experiences through imaginative play supports the development of narrative thought, the ability to see from other perspectives, and symbolic thinking.

Being willing to have a go refers to the child finding an interest, initiating activities, seeking challenge, having a 'can do' orientation, being willing to take a risk in new experiences, and developing the view of failures as opportunities to learn.

Active learning - motivation

Being involved and concentrating describes the intensity of attention that arises from children concentrating on following a line of interest in their activities.

Keeping on trying refers to the importance of persistence even in the face of challenge or difficulties, an element of purposeful control which supports resilience.

Enjoying achieving what they set out to do refers to the reward of meeting one's own goals, building on the intrinsic motivation which supports long-term success, rather than relying on the approval of others.

Creating and thinking critically - thinking

Having their own ideas covers the critical area of creativity - generating new ideas and approaches in all areas of endeavour. Being inventive allows children to find new problems as they seek challenge, and to explore ways of solving these.

Using what they already know to learn new things refers to the way in which children develop and link concepts, find meaning in sequence, cause and effect and in the intentions of others through both narrative and scientific modes of thought.

Choosing ways to do things and finding new ways involves approaching goal-directed activity in organised ways making choices and decisions about how to approach tasks, planning and monitoring what to do and being able to change strategies.

4.5 Reporting the EYFS Profile assessment

All EYFS providers completing the EYFS Profile must give parents a written summary of their child's attainment using the 17 ELGs and a narrative on how a child demonstrates the three characteristics of effective learning.

Year 1 teachers must be given a copy of the EYFS Profile report together with a narrative on how the child demonstrates the three characteristics of effective learning.

All EYFS providers must report EYFS Profile data (the 17 ELGs) to their LA for each child, upon request. The narrative on how a child demonstrates the three characteristics of effective learning should not be submitted.

Some children may have attended a range of settings during the final year of the EYFS. In these cases the EYFS Profile must be completed by the provider where the child spends the majority of their time between 8.00am and 6.00pm. If a child starts at a new setting before the summer half-term holiday, the new setting must report the child's results to the LA. If a child changes setting during the second half of the summer term then the previous setting is responsible for reporting to the LA. Providers should consider all available records of any formal or informal discussions with parents and others involved with the child during the previous year.

Reports should be specific to the child, concise and informative. They may include details from ongoing assessment and details from any other assessments appropriate to the individual child in order to help to identify the appropriate next steps in learning.

Detailed requirements around completion of the Profile, and reporting and informing parents about their child's progress are set out in the ARA.

5. Exemplification of 'expected' descriptors

5.1 Introduction

The exemplification on the Department's website at www.education.gov.uk/assessment establishes the national standard for the level of learning and development expected at the end of EYFS for each of the 17 ELGs of the EYFS Profile. It provides a single point of reference for:

- practitioners to make accurate judgements for each child's attainment;
- moderators to assess the accuracy of practitioner judgements;
- year 1 teachers to use EYFS Profile outcomes to plan effective provision; and
- other stakeholders who wish to evaluate children's learning and development.

Practitioners should use the exemplification to inform their decisions as to whether a child has met the level of development expected at the end of the EYFS for each ELG, has exceeded that level or not yet reached it (emerging).

The exemplification includes a variety of evidence and forms of presentation in order to demonstrate the wide range of ways in which information may be gathered to support EYFS Profile judgements. The material includes 'one off' observations, samples of children's work, photographs and contributions from parents. Some examples are part of a collection of material for an individual child or a group of children. There is no prescribed method of gathering evidence as a foundation for EYFS Profile judgements, nor any expectation that evidence should be recorded in this way. There are many methods of recording a child's attainment not included in this exemplification for practical reasons (for example video recordings). Practitioners will also build up a significant professional knowledge of each child which will not be recorded but which must be considered when EYFS Profile judgements are made.

The exemplification should not be regarded as either exclusive or inclusive of any child, no matter what their background or family circumstances. It is intended to be used without bias, preference or discrimination and schools and practitioners must ensure that they operate within all aspects of the statutory EYFS framework.

5.2 How to use the exemplification

In order to make judgements about attainment for each ELG, the practitioner must be familiar with the description of the area of learning and that of the level of development expected at the end of the EYFS. These set the context for practitioner judgement and the level of attainment which is expected for each child by the end of the EYFS. Practitioners should also be familiar with the developmental continuum leading to each ELG. Practitioners can ensure their judgements are accurate and consistent by considering each child's learning and development in the light of:

- the area of learning; and
- the level of development expected at the end of EYFS for each ELG, informed by the exemplification.

When completing an EYFS Profile, practitioners are asked to make a best-fit judgement for each ELG using the description of learning and development expected at the end of the EYFS. When making a decision, practitioners must consider the entirety of each ELG. To create the most accurate picture of the child's overall embedded learning, a holistic view of the descriptor should be taken. Sections of each descriptor must not be seen in isolation.

When viewing each set of exemplification it is important to understand that the set as a whole illustrates the 'expected' descriptor. No one piece of evidence meets the ELG as a standalone item; together they illustrate the pitch and breadth of a particular 'expected' level of learning and development.

The prime and specific areas of learning, the aspects of learning and their associated ELGs are set out below. Exemplification material should always be viewed in the context of a specific aspect of learning in order to retain an accurate focus. However, practitioners should be aware that a child's learning and development are not compartmentalised and a focus on one aspect of learning will shed light on several other related areas.

Exemplification of the expected descriptions is available on the Department's website at www.education.gov.uk/assessment.

5.3 Areas and aspects of learning of EYFS and their associated ELGs

For all the ELGs except speaking, the principle that a child can use their established or preferred mode of communication holds true. In this case additional detail around their understanding and preferred means of communication should accompany their profile record.

EYFS areas of learning and their associated ELGs

Prime areas of learning	
Communication and language development involves giving children opportunities to speak and listen in a range of situations and to develop their confidence and skills in expressing themselves.	
ELG 01	**Listening and attention:** Children listen attentively in a range of situations. They listen to stories, accurately anticipating key events, and respond to what they hear with relevant comments, questions or actions. They give their attention to what others say and respond appropriately, while engaged in another activity.
ELG 02	**Understanding:** Children follow instructions involving several ideas or actions. They answer 'how' and 'why' questions about their experiences and in response to stories or events.
ELG 03	**Speaking:** Children express themselves effectively, showing awareness of listeners' needs. They use past, present and future forms accurately when talking about events that have happened or are to happen in the future. They develop their own narratives and explanations by connecting ideas or events.
Physical development involves providing opportunities for young children to be active and interactive, and to develop their co-ordination, control, and movement. Children must also be helped to understand the importance of physical activity, and to make healthy choices in relation to food.	
ELG 04	**Moving and handling:** Children show good control and co-ordination in large and small movements. They move confidently in a range of ways, safely negotiating space. They handle equipment and tools effectively, including pencils for writing.
ELG 05	**Health and self-care:** Children know the importance for good health of physical exercise and a healthy diet, and talk about ways to keep healthy and safe. They manage their own basic hygiene and personal needs successfully, including dressing and going to the toilet independently.
Personal, social and emotional development involves helping children to develop a positive sense of themselves and others; to form positive relationships and develop respect for others; to develop social skills and learn how to manage their feelings; to understand appropriate behaviour in groups; and to have confidence in their own abilities.	
ELG 06	**Self-confidence and self-awareness:** Children are confident to try new activities, and to say why they like some activities more than others. They are confident to speak in a familiar group, will talk about their ideas, and will choose the resources they need for their chosen activities. They say when they do or do not need help.
ELG 07	**Managing feelings and behaviour:** Children talk about how they and others show feelings, talk about their own and others' behaviour, and its consequences, and know that some behaviour is unacceptable. They work as part of a group or class, and understand and follow rules. They adjust their behaviour to different situations, and take changes of routine in their stride.

	Prime areas of learning
ELG 08	**Making relationships:** Children play cooperatively, taking turns with others. They take account of one another's ideas about how to organise their activity. They show sensitivity to others' needs and feelings, and form positive relationships with adults and other children.

	Specific areas of learning
	Literacy development involves encouraging children to read and write, both through listening to others reading, and being encouraged to begin to read and write themselves. Children must be given access to a wide range of reading materials – for example books, poems, and other materials to ignite their interest.
ELG 09	**Reading:** Children read and understand simple sentences. They use phonic knowledge to decode regular words and read them aloud accurately. They also read some common irregular words. They demonstrate an understanding when talking with others about what they have read.
ELG 10	**Writing:** Children use their phonic knowledge to write words in ways which match their spoken sounds. They also write some irregular common words. They write sentences which can be read by themselves and others. Some words are spelt correctly and others are phonetically plausible.
	Mathematics development involves providing children with opportunities to practise and improve their skills in counting numbers, calculating simple addition and subtraction problems, and to describe shapes, spaces, and measures.
ELG 11	**Numbers:** Children count reliably with numbers from one to 20, place them in order and say which number is one more or one less than a given number. Using quantities and objects, they add and subtract two single-digit numbers and count on or back to find the answer. They solve problems, including doubling, halving and sharing.
ELG 12	**Shape, space and measures:** Children use everyday language to talk about size, weight, capacity, position, distance, time and money to compare quantities and objects and to solve problems. They recognise, create and describe patterns. They explore characteristics of everyday objects and shapes and use mathematical language to describe them.
	Understanding of the world involves guiding children to make sense of their physical world and their community through opportunities to explore, observe and find out about people, places, technology and the environment.

Specific areas of learning	
ELG 13	**People and communities:** Children talk about past and present events in their own lives and in the lives of family members. They know that other children do not always enjoy the same things, and are sensitive to this. They know about similarities and differences between themselves and others, and among families, communities and traditions.
ELG 14	**The world:** Children know about similarities and differences in relation to places, objects, materials and living things. They talk about the features of their own immediate environment and how environments might vary from one another. They make observations of animals and plants and explain why some things occur, and talk about changes.
ELG 15	**Technology:** Children recognise that a range of technology is used in places such as homes and schools. They select and use technology for particular purposes.
Expressive arts and design involves supporting children to explore and play with a wide range of media and materials, as well as providing opportunities and encouragement for sharing their thoughts, ideas and feelings through a variety of activities in art, music, movement, dance, role play, and design and technology.	
ELG 16	**Exploring and using media and materials:** Children sing songs, make music and dance, and experiment with ways of changing them. They safely use and explore a variety of materials, tools and techniques, experimenting with colour, design, texture, form and function.
ELG 17	**Being imaginative:** Children use what they have learnt about media and materials in original ways, thinking about uses and purposes. They represent their own ideas, thoughts and feelings through design and technology, art, music, dance, role play and stories.

6. Moderation of the EYFS Profile

6.1 Purpose of moderation

Local authorities are responsible for providing a robust moderation process so that practitioner judgements are evaluated in line with statutory requirements.

The purpose of moderation is to:

- secure the consistency and accuracy of judgements made by different practitioners;
- reassure practitioners that their judgements are accurate, valid and consistent with national standards; and
- assure moderators that an acceptable level of accuracy and validity has been achieved for assessments recorded and reported by the settings for which they have responsibility.

Moderation of the EYFS Profile is a sampling process – unlike testing – and so it is not a method for checking each child's attainment. LA moderation visits check teachers' ability to make accurate assessments and apply them consistently.

Moderation involves both internal moderation activities and professional discussion between moderators and practitioners. This is to ensure that practitioners' judgements are consistent with national standards and the assessment process is reliable, accurate and secure.

The EYFS Profile provides an holistic picture of a child's attainment at the end of the EYFS in relation to the ELGs. Everyone needs to feel confident that the recorded judgements are fair and consistent for all children so that judgements made for any one child are comparable with those made for all children. Processes to achieve comparability will involve practitioners working with each other throughout the year alongside an annual programme of agreement activity within each LA.

The starting point for the agreement of judgements should be the ELGs illustrating the level of development expected at the end of the EYFS for each ELG and their exemplification. Practitioners will need to work with each other and with LA moderators to achieve consistent understanding of the ELGs so that comparable best fit judgements can be made.

6.2 Internal moderation

The moderation of EYFS Profile assessments begins within each individual setting and is supported by local authorities or LA approved agencies through a programme of visits and meetings. Within their own settings, practitioners can agree assessment judgements with others. Informally, this might involve two practitioners, for example a teacher and a teaching assistant or a Reception class teacher and a year 1 teacher, discussing an observation about a child's development.

A more formal agreement process might take place during staff meetings and/or staff training days. An example could be discussion of planned paired observations or the

development of a group of children in relation to one of the ELGs. The focus for this planned work should be clear and manageable. LA moderators will support this work during visits or meetings.

6.3 Inter-school moderation

It is important for practitioners to build a shared understanding of the ELGs and the national exemplification of standards and to discuss their assessment of children's attainment with colleagues. Settings may wish to collaborate so that practitioners from a range of different settings can share experience to develop their assessment skills. Outcomes of discussions could be recorded and referenced during moderation visits.

6.4 Local authority requirements for moderation

Section 13 of the Childcare Act 2006 requires local authorities to secure the provision of information, advice and training, whether delivered by themselves or by others, to meet the needs of local providers and support the sufficiency of childcare provision. Regulations made under this section include ensuring that:

- training in EYFS assessment and the completion of the EYFS Profile summaries is offered to all providers who require it;
- EYFS Profile assessment judgements are moderated;
- local authorities appoint and train moderators with appropriate experience of the EYFS and the ELGs to secure consistent standards in assessment judgements; and
- all providers are visited regularly as part of a cycle of moderation visits, and notified about whether the EYFS Profile assessment is being carried out in accordance with requirements.

Where the LA moderator judges that the assessment is not in line with the exemplified standards, the LA can require the provider to arrange for the practitioner to participate in further training or moderation activities, and to reconsider their assessments as advised by the moderator.

Moderation focuses on a professional discussion between moderators and practitioners in order to ensure that practitioner judgements are consistent with the national exemplification of standards, and that the assessment of attainment is reliable, accurate and secure. Local authorities must moderate all 17 ELGs annually in a minimum of 25 per cent of all settings which implement the EYFS Profile.

LA moderation consists of the validation of practitioner judgements within visits carried out by a suitably experienced and trained moderator external to the setting.

All practitioners implementing the EYFS Profile are required to take part in either a moderation visit or EYFS Profile training (including agreement trialling activities) each year. Visits will take place on a four-year cycle within each LA. Specific guidance about moderation measurements, including the requirements for academies can be found in the ARA.

Local authorities should inform settings that are to receive an EYFS Profile moderation visit by the end of the spring term. For moderation purposes, these settings will need to complete interim judgements against all the ELGs at the beginning of May for children in the final year of the EYFS. Individual settings can be added to the LA sample after this date, if particular issues arise.

6.5 STA external moderation of local authority moderation models

To fulfill its remit, STA visits a number of local authorities during the summer term, in order to undertake external moderation of their approaches and procedures. A representative sample of local authorities will be visited each year.

The role of STA's external moderators is to visit the local authorities that make up the annual national sample, and to examine approaches to implementation and moderation of the EYFS Profile by:

- attending a moderation visit undertaken by the LA;
- meeting with the EYFS Profile moderation manager and appropriate personnel to discuss the approaches to moderation, training and support; and
- reporting to STA on the quality of the LA's approaches to moderation and the robustness of the model employed.

6.6 Moderation training cycle

Training will focus on all 17 ELGs of the Profile over a three-year cycle, set out in the table below. This training should be in addition to support provided by the LA for newly qualified teachers (NQTs) and those new to Reception.

School year	Moderation visits	Moderation training and ELG focus
2013/14	25% of settings (minimum)	75% of practitioners not receiving a moderation visit (minimum) **Prime area of learning:** Communication and language development **Specific area of learning:** Mathematics Training should include the opportunity for agreement trialling.
2014/15	25% of settings (minimum)	75% of practitioners not receiving a moderation visit (minimum) **Prime area of learning:** Physical development **Specific area of learning:** Understanding the world and expressive arts and design Training should include the opportunity for agreement trialling.

School year	Moderation visits	Moderation training and ELG focus
2015/16	25% of settings (minimum)	75% of practitioners not receiving a moderation visit (minimum) **Prime area of learning:** Personal , social and emotional development **Specific area of learning:** Literacy Training should include the opportunity for agreement trialling.
2016/17	25% of settings (minimum)	75% of practitioners not receiving a moderation visit (minimum) **Prime area of learning:** Communication and language development **Specific area of learning:** Mathematics Training should include the opportunity for agreement trialling.

6.7 The moderation of children with outcomes in the 'emerging' band

The purpose of moderation is the validation or otherwise of practitioner judgements. Where these judgements are that the child is at an 'emerging' level of development, the moderation discussion must reference both the description of the expected level of development (the ELG) and the child's previous development continuum so that the practitioner's understanding and application of the threshold between an 'emerging' and 'expected' outcome can be evaluated.

This evaluation must be applied on an individual ELG basis. There will be many children with SEND who are at the 'expected' or 'exceeding' level of development for some goals, and at an 'emerging' level for those goals where their specific condition has an impact on their learning and development. There will also be children for whom outcomes at the end of EYFS as captured by the EYFS Profile will be at the 'emerging' level for all ELG and it is important that moderation of such a pattern of outcome is a meaningful process.

> Moderation should maintain its purpose of evaluating the accuracy of practitioner judgements at individual ELG level whatever the pattern of a child's EYFS Profile outcomes

Where an outcome of 'emerging' appears clear-cut, and limited moderation discussion may be required to ascertain accuracy of a best-fit judgement, moderation should aim to ensure that the characteristic of effective learning narrative highlights those aspects of the child's learning and development which may be masked by the 17 ELG outcomes.

For children with SEND, practitioners will seek to provide such additional detail as is needed to support successful transition to year 1 and enable the year 1 teacher to plan an effective, responsive and appropriate curriculum. Consideration of some of this information within the moderation discussion will strengthen the outcome of moderation, by focussing on the holistic picture of the child and the professional knowledge of the practitioner, and support the development of a shared understanding of how the EYFS Profile can be used to support successful transition for children with SEND.

Discussion between a moderator and practitioner may be especially helpful where a child's specific circumstances are such that their development does not follow a linear path so that making a best-fit judgement as to their level of learning and development may be both problematic and of limited meaning.

6.8 The moderation of children with outcomes in the 'exceeding' band

The purpose of moderation is the validation or otherwise of practitioner judgements. Where these judgements are that the child is at an 'exceeding' level of development, the moderation discussion must reference both the description of the expected level of development (the ELG) and refer to key stage 1 attainment targets and level descriptors together with the 'exceeding' descriptors (sourced from the Tickell review) as per Annex 2.

This process must be applied on an individual ELG basis, and there may be children whose learning and development is at an 'exceeding' level for some goals and at an 'expected' level for others.

Where this is the case, a differentiated curriculum should be planned to ensure there is enough challenge to extend the child's learning within a practical, relevant and meaningful environment in all 17 ELGs rather than channeling the child's learning in one or two ELGs.

Regardless of any internal school arrangements, an EYFS profile must be completed for the child in line with statutory reporting requirements.

6.9 The moderation sample

Moderation is about reviewing a sample of completed profiles to establish whether the practitioner has understood what constitutes an appropriate outcome and the thresholds between them in order to make accurate judgements.

If the moderator is not confident in the practitioners' judgements s/he may increase the sample of completed profiles. The moderator must ensure s/he sees enough to be confident in the practitioners' accuracy.

It is not a prescriptive process but requires the professional knowledge and experience of the moderator. Where practitioners are released for parts of the moderation visit, it may be helpful for one member of staff to be present for the whole of the visit.

In single form entry schools moderators will moderate 17 ELGs from one practitioner. The moderator will expect to see some 'emerging', some 'expected' and some 'exceeding' outcomes from across the five children.

In a multi form entry school the moderator will ensure that all 17 ELGs are moderated across the sample from the school with at least one judgement at each of the three outcome levels from each practitioner within that sample.

There may be some overlap to confirm accuracy of judgements, for example ELG 02: Understanding may be scrutinised at 'expected' in one class and 'exceeding' in another. Any combination/link could be used to ensure moderator confidence.

6.10 Key elements of an effective moderation process

The following table sets out the requirements for robust LA moderation processes and procedures, and identifies key elements and examples of the most effective practice. The requirements, set out across the top of each section, draw on the Statutory framework for the EYFS, (published in March 2012), which is available from the Department's website at www.education.gov.uk/assessment.

The sections in the table below can be cross referenced with the planning forms that STA send annually to all local authorities.

Local authorities must have regard to guidance produced by STA, exercising their powers and duties in the way the guidance sets out. Where a LA chooses to undertake a moderation model not reliant on moderation visits, it must ensure it can demonstrate that all the key elements of the moderation visit are protected. Any deviation which does not have regard to STA's guidance would be deemed as not meeting statutory requirements.

A: Moderation plan	
The LA should plan an annual programme to ensure that their statutory duty in relation to the moderation of the EYFS Profile judgements is met.	
Key elements	**Examples of most effective practice**

• Before implementation, details of the moderation plan are shared and agreed with all settings which will complete EYFS Profiles.
 	
• The moderation plan includes a specific appeals procedure in relation to the moderation of EYFS Profile judgements. (In the event that an appeal remains unresolved, the LA moderation manager must notify STA for information purposes only.)
 	
• The moderation process is evaluated each year in consultation with all stakeholders. The plan is revised accordingly.
	• Details of the moderation process are communicated to all relevant stakeholders early in the autumn term.
	
	• The stakeholder group includes:
	  • LA colleagues
	  • headteachers/managers of settings
	  • practitioners
	  • moderation team
	  • LA data teams

B: Moderation team	
In order to carry out the statutory role of moderator, the moderation team should have a thorough understanding and experience of the principles and practice of the EYFS Profile and appropriate experience of the EYFS.	
Key elements	**Examples of most effective practice**
• The moderation team includes both LA personnel and serving practitioners with appropriate and recent EYFS experience. • Moderators are recruited who have the appropriate skills and capabilities to carry out their role • Moderators are trained and participate regularly in LA moderation activities, using exemplification of national standards to ensure consistency. • The LA has an effective process for the recruitment of new moderators as appropriate. • Moderators new to the role undertake a suitable induction process.	• All moderators undertake the full range of moderation activity. • The recruitment process allows for all interested parties to apply. (A suggested role description for moderators can be found in Annex 4.) • As part of their induction newly appointed moderators have access to a mentor and opportunities to shadow a more experienced colleague.

C: Inter-authority moderation	
LA moderators will need to work with other moderators so that assessment is consistent nationally.	
Key elements	**Examples of most effective practice**
• The moderation manager participates regularly in inter-LA moderation activities.	• All moderators participate regularly in inter-LA moderation activities, using exemplification of national standards to ensure consistency. • Pairing arrangements between moderators from different local authorities provide opportunities for the promotion of consistency.

D: Moderation cycle	
Local authorities should ensure that all 17 ELGs of the EYFS Profile are moderated annually in a 25 per cent sample of settings. All practitioners responsible for the completion of the EYFS Profile who are not receiving a moderation visit must take part in training which includes an element of agreement trialling.	
Key elements	**Examples of most effective practice**

• All settings receive a moderation visit on a four-year cycle.
 	
• All 17 ELGs of the EYFS Profile are moderated annually: moderation does not focus on a specific area of learning or set of ELGs at the expense of others.
 	
• All practitioners responsible for the completion of the EYFS Profile who are not receiving a moderation visit in the current year must take part in training which includes an element of agreement trialling.
 	
• Moderation visits take place during the summer term.
	• The moderation cycle includes opportunities for supportive visits throughout the year as preparation for the final moderation visit, during which the accuracy of judgements is established.
	
	• In addition to planned visits to all settings on a four-year cycle, moderation visits/support may be triggered by:
	  ○ presence of NQTs and practitioners new to the EYFS
	  ○ requests from the headteacher/manager
	  ○ concerns identified by the school improvement partner or LA personnel
	  ○ data anomalies
	  ○ non-attendance at training events.

E: Moderation visits to schools and settings

As part of their statutory duty for moderation, local authorities are required to visit schools and settings implementing the EYFS Profile on a regular basis. This should be on a four-year cycle so that 25 per cent of practitioners responsible for the completion of the EYFS Profile are visited each year.

Key elements	Examples of most effective practice
• The moderation visit focuses on a professional discussion between the moderator and each practitioner responsible for completing EYFS Profiles. • Local authorities ensure that practitioners are familiar with STA guidance materials and moderators reference these where relevant during the moderation visit. • For each ELG the moderator establishes whether EYFS Profile assessment has been undertaken in accordance with statutory requirements and is in line with exemplified national standards • Visits take place at an agreed time within the school day, with practitioners released for the duration of the visit. • The moderator establishes the accuracy and consistency of practitioner judgements by scrutinising a range of evidence, the majority of which will come from the practitioner's knowledge of the child and observations of the child's self-initiated activities. Moderators must not scrutinise recorded evidence without the practitioner present. • At the time of the visit, the practitioner provides the moderator with a list of the EYFS Profile interim outcomes for each child. The moderator selects five complete profiles across the range of attainment ('emerging', 'expected' and 'exceeding'). These will form the basis of the moderation discussion. • The moderator must ensure that within the constraints of the range of attainment available, practitioner judgements for all 17 ELGs are moderated. The moderator is unlikely to scrutinise all 17 ELGs for all five children, but will ensure that judgements are moderated from each of the three outcome bands ('emerging', 'expected' and 'exceeding').	• Information meetings are held for settings that are to receive a moderation visit prior to visits taking place. • The headteacher/manager, senior leadership team, subject leaders and year 1 teachers have opportunities to participate in elements of the moderation visit. • Contributions from parents and the child are actively sought by practitioners; and are used to inform the judgements made for the EYFS Profile. • The LA has an effective system to follow up any advised actions. An example visit note can be found in Annex 5. • When moderating EYFS Profile judgements in multiple form entry schools, moderators must ensure that all practitioners participate in the moderation discussion. Moderators should ensure that the judgements moderated cover all 17 ELGs including judgements from all three attainment bands for each class. Moderators should adjust the size of the sample as appropriate to ensure that this can be achieved.

E: Moderation visits (continued)	
Key elements	**Examples of most effective practice**
• Information concerning the characteristics of effective learning are an integral part of the moderation discussion being carried out in accordance with statutory requirements and whether practitioner judgements are accurate.	
• Moderators ensure that judgements are validated throughout the professional discussion.	
• Outcomes of internal and cross-school moderation are considered within the moderation discussion. Moderators establish how settings develop and use internal moderation processes.	
• At the end of the visit, the moderator informs the headteacher/manager of the outcome of moderation.	
• Where the moderator judges that the assessment is not in line with exemplification of national standards, the LA can require the headteacher/ manager to both reconsider the practitioner's judgements as advised by the moderator and arrange further CPD opportunities for the practitioner.	
• Moderators refer to all the documents required to explore and validate exceeding judgements including the national curriculum key stage 1 attainment targets and level descriptors.	

F: Specific EYFS Profile training	
Specific training, which includes agreement trialling, is provided annually to ensure that EYFS Profile assessments are in line with the requirements set out in the EYFS statutory framework.	
Key elements	**Examples of most effective practice**
<ul><li>Specific EYFS Profile training, which includes agreement trialling, is provided for practitioners responsible for the completion of the EYFS Profile in the 75 per cent of settings not receiving a moderation visit.</li><li>Moderators support agreement trialling activities during training.</li><li>The LA has a system in place to follow up concerns raised by the moderators during agreement trialling activities.</li><li>Training focuses on all 17 ELGs over a three-year cycle.</li><li>Exemplification of national standards is used to support training and ensure national consistency with regard to the principles and processes of EYFS profile assessment and the accuracy of judgements.</li><li>Systems are in place to monitor the attendance at all training events and non-attendance is followed up where appropriate.</li></ul>	<ul><li>Additional training is provided, specific to the context and needs of the LA.</li><li>Within the LA there is an expectation that all stakeholders will attend training in order to ensure their knowledge and understanding of the EYFS Profile is up to date.</li><li>The agreement trialling element of the training focusses on the practitioner's own evidence which has informed their judgements.</li><li>Invitations to training are extended to other practitioners e.g. year 1 teachers, assessment leaders, headteachers/ managers and subject co-ordinators.</li><li>Outcomes of agreement trialling are recorded.</li></ul>

G: Data collection and analysis

Local authorities are required to collect EYFS Profile data by Friday 20 June. This collection (and subsequent return to the Department where required) should be carried out in line with the ARA.

Key elements	Examples of most effective practice
• All EYFS providers have an appropriate system to record and submit EYFS Profile data. • The LA informs all settings of the advised EYFS profile completion window (Monday 9 June to Friday 20 June 2014) and makes appropriate arrangements for the submission of data. • The LA moderation manager has an effective working relationship with both the LA, IT and data analysis teams. Systems for the collection, submission and analysis of EYFS Profile data are evaluated and developed each year.	• Local authorities provide a helpdesk or other means of support for the data collection system, and training is provided for any personnel new to the process.

H: Quality assurance of EYFS Profile data

Settings and local authorities should have quality assurance processes in place to ensure that the data submitted for each child is an accurate reflection of their attainment.

Key elements	Examples of most effective practice
• Headteachers/managers take responsibility for the reliability of the EYFS Profile outcomes and ensure that the data accurately reflects the attainment of their cohort of children. • The LA has an effective process for the quality assurance of EYFS Profile data prior to submission to the Department. EYFS Profile data from settings is scrutinised by the moderation manager and the LA data team. • The LA allocates adequate time for the quality assurance of data prior to submission to the Department. • The LA scrutinises data at a level of detail that enables anomalies to be identified and highlighted to settings for review and amendment (where necessary). • Amendments to EYFS Profile outcomes are made prior to submission to the Department.	• The exploration of anomalies reflects an understanding of local circumstances and priorities. Any sampling of data for scrutiny takes place with regard to local intelligence. • Systems for the quality assurance of EYFS Profile data are evaluated and developed each year. • The need for accuracy in EYFS Profile data is embedded in training for all stakeholders.

I: Use of data to support planning in year 1	
One of the main purposes of the EYFS Profile is to inform the year 1 teacher of the attainment of each child. This will enable the teacher to plan an effective, responsive and appropriate curriculum that will meet children's needs.	
Key elements	**Examples of most effective practice**
• Opportunities are provided to help year 1 teachers understand and use EYFS Profile data effectively so that they can plan a curriculum that meets the needs of all children. • Year 1 teachers participate in internal EYFS Profile moderation within the school. • Training is provided for year 1 teachers focussed on the understanding and interpretation of EYFS Profile outcomes and how these may be used to support transition, provision and planning in year 1.	• Transition processes are developed and evaluated each year in response to EYFS Profile outcomes, in order to reflect the needs of the current cohort. • Year 1 teachers participate in LA moderation visits and training events.

7. Quality assurance of the EYFS Profile

EYFS Profile data must be sufficiently reliable and accurate to meet its purposes (see section 2.1). There are a number of quality assurance activities to ensure that there is accurate, reliable and valid information that can be used to improve outcomes for all children. These include:

- teachers and practitioners meeting within a school and between schools or settings, to develop a consistent understanding of the ELGs;
- external moderation visits organised by the LA; and
- a quality assurance review by the LA after data has been submitted.

Quality assurance of EYFS Profile data has two main elements:

- to ensure that the pattern of outcomes for an individual child makes sense in relation to wider knowledge of children's learning and development; and
- to ensure that the resulting data is an accurate record of practitioner judgements.

Practitioners, school managers, setting leaders and local authorities have responsibility for ensuring the quality, accuracy and reliability of data arising from EYFS Profile assessment.

7.1 The pattern of outcomes for an individual child

The moderation process includes considering the pattern of attainment for children in the selected sample. Local authorities are responsible for providing a robust moderation process so that practitioner judgements are evaluated in line with statutory requirements. It is important that settings carry out a 'sense check' of outcomes for all children for whom an EYFS Profile judgement has been made, so that an accurate picture of their learning and development is provided for parents and year 1 teachers.

Consideration of any EYFS Profile outcome must include both the judgements against the ELG statement of the level of development expected at the end of the EYFS, and the narrative record of the child's characteristics of effective learning. It is the information contained within the narrative for the characteristics of effective learning which will enable the patterns of attainment to be placed in the necessary context so that the accuracy of the EYFS Profile outcome can be evaluated effectively.

The following statements could support level setting quality assurance processes in terms of scrutiny of the pattern of attainment for individual children. Each child's pattern of attainment will reflect their learning and development outcomes. Where this pattern does not match what might be anticipated, the prompts may provide a starting point for a discussion with the practitioner making the judgement. An unexpected pattern of attainment, however, does not necessarily mean that any individual child's EYFS Profile outcomes are inaccurate, as the following examples demonstrate.

1. A child's outcomes are consistently exceeding ELGs but the characteristics of effective learning describe a child who lacks interest and excitement to learn. Whilst this scenario is possible, high attainment is often associated with interest in learning. It is essential to link the commentary within the characteristics of effective learning to the attainment of the ELGs.

2. A child's ability to communicate effectively threads through many of the ELGs. A child whose outcome for Speaking is at the 'emerging' level may also show 'emerging' attainment for those ELGs with a significant communication element. These include Self-confidence and self-awareness; Managing feelings and behaviour; Understanding; Shape, space and measures; People and communities and Knowledge of the world.

3. A child meets the level of development expected at the end of EYFS for Reading but does not do so for Listening and attention. The Reading ELG includes elements which rest upon a child using significant skills relating to listening and attention.

4. A child meets the level of development expected at the end of the EYFS for Writing but does not do so for Physical development (moving and handling). While the ability to hold and manipulate a pencil effectively is only part of the Physical ELG, a child whose physical development in relation to fine motor movements is at the 'emerging' level may not be a confident and independent writer as expressed by the Writing ELG.

5. Some elements of the Expressive arts ELGs depend on a child's physical ability to explore and manipulate media with confidence, including construction materials. A child with 'emerging' physical (moving and handling) skills may not attain the level of development expected at the end of the EYFS in relation to these creative ELGs.

6. A child who is at the level of development expected at the end of the EYFS for Shape, space and measures and Knowledge of the world is likely to be using the skills and attributes which would contribute towards attainment of the level of development expected at the end of the EYFS for Understanding.

It should be remembered throughout quality assurance that children with specific SEND may be assessed in relation to their ability to communicate, for example, without the need for speech. Any exploration of patterns of attainment should take into account the contextual information for individual children which underpin accurate assessment.

7.2 The role of settings in quality assurance

Schools and settings have responsibility for ensuring the quality, accuracy and reliability of data arising from EYFS Profile assessment; practitioners have a central role to play in ensuring that judgements are reliable and accurate. Practitioners need to be familiar with the ELGs and their exemplification if they are to apply them consistently.

In each school, Early Years practitioners and year 1 teachers should work together to build a consistent, shared understanding of what the ELGs mean via internal moderation activities. Practitioners in groups of schools may also wish to work together in this way.

It is particularly important that year 1 teachers understand the EYFS Profile, so that they can make effective use of it to inform their teaching. Year 1 teachers should be encouraged to play a role as moderators.

Headteachers and managers have responsibility within their settings for the accuracy of EYFS Profile outcomes. They should be actively involved in the quality assurance process within the setting prior to submission to the LA, and later if the LA quality assurance process generates enquiries.

7.3 Data entry and submission

Accurate data entry relies on good communication and shared understanding between those providing information and those responsible for entering and transmitting the resulting data.

The EYFS Profile is a statutory data collection. Each child's records are combined at setting, LA and national level to produce a data set which has national statistics status and informs a range of processes.

The process of data collection, entry and submission should be planned in advance, with sufficient time included for the resolution of queries and visual checking of data once entered. Understanding and recognition of common input errors is vital. It is therefore essential that local authorities give clear information to settings so that they understand how data should be formatted.

Efficient and high quality data submission relies on several features and processes, each of which should be established within the setting to ensure accuracy from the outset. These are set out below:

1. An understanding of settings' systems for the recording of children's profile outcomes and the submission of the data to the LA.

2. Clear recording by the practitioner.

3. Understanding of the nature of EYFS Profile data by all those responsible for data collection and submission.

4. Accurate transcription of data from setting record to electronic record.

5. Checking of entered data against that originally provided by the practitioner.

6. Accurate and updated recording of children's information which accompanies EYFS Profile data, for example postcode and unique pupil number (UPN).

7. Final checking and sign-off by the headteacher/manager prior to submission to the LA.

The headteacher/manager should only sign off item level data, and permit onward transmission to the LA, after checking that there are no input errors and the data is an accurate reflection of the attainment of the cohort.

7.4 Local authority review of submitted data

Once EYFS Profile data is received by the LA, the validity and accuracy of that data should be scrutinised by both moderation and data professionals so that an accurate local data set is prepared for onward submission to the Department. The focus of scrutiny may be different for each of these teams, but there is likely to be overlap and best practice will result from combined processes with shared responsibility.

Local authorities should explain their quality assurance processes to settings early in the data collection cycle. This will ensure timescales and expectations are well established, and appropriate activity planned at setting and LA level. Timings should allow for:

- scrutiny by LA data and moderation teams;
- the raising of enquiries with settings;
- the resolution of these enquiries; and
- the submission of amended data if required.

Data passes from local authorities to the Department via the COLLECT data collection system. Data collection requirements include timescales for submission and a range of validation checks which data must pass in order to be accepted by the Department. These are the subject of discussion between the Department and local authorities. The Department provides clear information regarding expectations and processes annually ahead of the national data collection. Data validation ensures the alpha-numerical consistency of specific data items.

Beyond data validation, LA moderation managers should seek to ensure that the local EYFS Profile data set presents an accurate picture of children's learning and development at the end of the EYFS within their LA. This could include a range of measures to check a further sample of outcomes, or a cross checking of outcomes against those anticipated as a result of moderation. The nature of any sampling should be transparent and shared with settings prior to data collection.

The following questions may support local authorities when considering the accuracy of their EYFS Profile data set prior to submission to the Department.

1. Does the setting's data reflect LA knowledge of the cohort or outcomes of moderation?

2. Is there a difference in data between classes where there is multiple form entry?

3. Is the setting's data significantly or unexpectedly adrift from LA data?

4. Are there patterns of attainment which are unexpected in terms of what is known about children's learning and development in general?

5. Are trends from year to year unexpected?

Effective quality assurance rests on knowledge both of EYFS Profile assessment and of the schools and settings which are returning data. As set out in section 6.2 above, these questions are prompts for a discussion rather than rules which data must obey. Quality assurance may also include a 'first cut' data analysis and feedback from the LA to the setting, which may be beneficial for a setting's internal evaluation and transition processes.

If moderation managers highlight a potential inconsistency in a setting's data set, they must ensure that headteachers/managers have enough time to discuss the data with setting staff and provide a response in sufficient detail to resolve the enquiry. Where data needs to be amended, clear arrangements must be in place to enable amendment, headteacher/manager sign-off and re-submission before the end of the summer term. This should be coordinated with the LA data team so that duplicate data sets are not created and the correctly amended data is included in the final local submission to the Department.

8. Glossary

Achievement
Takes account both of a child's attainment and progress over time.

Active learning
Refers to motivation comprising three aspects:

- being involved and concentrating
- keeping on trying
- enjoying achieving what they set out to do.

Agreement trialling
The process of discussing assessment judgements in a group in order to ensure that all practitioners understand the national exemplification of standards and apply them consistently.

Area of learning
Refers to the grouping of children's learning and development into seven areas. There are three prime areas which focus on the earliest experiences which are foundations for learning: Personal, social and emotional development, Communication and language and Physical development. There are four specific areas in which the prime skills are applied: Literacy, Mathematics, Expressive arts and design, and Understanding the world.

Aspect of learning
The strand of specific focus within an area of learning. For example, Personal, social and emotional development has three aspects: Self-confidence and self-awareness, Managing feelings and Behaviour and making relationships.

Assessment
Involves analysing and reviewing what is known about each child's learning and development to reach informed decisions about the child's level of attainment.

Attainment
What a child knows, understands and can do.

Best fit
Making a judgement as to whether the child's learning and development is best described by:

- the 'expected' description for each ELG;
- not yet at the expected level (emerging); or
- beyond the level expected at the end of the EYFS (exceeding).

To create the most accurate picture of the child's overall embedded learning an holistic view of the descriptor should be taken. Practitioners must consider the entirety of each ELG and avoid splitting the descriptor into sections.

Because children do not necessarily achieve uniformly, the practitioner should judge whether the description within the ELG best fits the child's learning and development, taking into account their relative strengths and weaknesses. 'Best fit' does not mean that the child has equal mastery or knowledge of all aspects of the ELG.

In making this decision, practitioners must refer to the exemplification of national standards. The exemplification illustrates the standard expected for each ELG at the end of the EYFS.

Characteristics of effective learning

The three characteristics of effective learning comprise playing and exploring, active learning and creating and thinking critically. The characteristics describe the different ways children learn rather than what they learn. They begin at birth and are lifelong characteristics which are critical for building children's capacity for future learning. These characteristics need to be understood by practitioners working across all seven areas of learning.

Child initiated

The action of a child choosing to extend, repeat or explore an activity. This activity may or may not have been introduced or prompted by an adult. It is the child's innovation within or of the activity which is important and relevant to child initiation. An adult may be present and may be supportive but not directive. For example an adult may be supporting the child to realise an idea by providing necessary resources, or by engaging in thought provoking conversation. Child initiated activity and exploration provides an important insight into the depth of a child's learning. When learning is fully mastered the child is able and motivated to employ that learning unprompted.

Creating and thinking critically

Refers to thinking comprising three aspects:

* having their own ideas;
* using what they already know to learn new things; and
* choosing ways to do things and finding new ways.

Early learning goal (ELG)

A collection of statements which sets out the expected level of attainment at the end of the EYFS. There are 17 ELGs drawn from seven areas of learning.

Embedded learning

The learning that is demonstrated without the need for overt adult support. Where learning is secure, at whatever level, it is likely that children often initiate the use of that learning. Judgements about this are made through observing behaviour that a child demonstrates consistently and independently in a range of situations. Attainment in this context will assure practitioners of the child's confidence and ownership of the specific knowledge, skill or concept being assessed. Skilful interactions with adults and learning which is supported by them are necessary on the journey to embedding skills and knowledge. However, demonstrations of attainment which are often dependent on adult support are not examples of fully acquired skills and knowledge and are not embedded learning.

Emerging development

Describes attainment at a level which has not reached that expressed by the ELGs. Practitioners should refer to the descriptors of age bands in Development matters to determine which age band best describes a child's development.

Evidence

Any material, knowledge of a child, specific anecdotal incident, observation or information from additional sources that supports the overall picture of a child's attainment. There is no expectation or requirement that such evidence is always formally recorded or documented. Practitioners may choose to record specific evidence in order to secure their own judgements.

'Expected' development
The development expected by the end of the EYFS and described by 17 ELGs drawn from seven areas of learning.

'Exceeding' development
Describes attainment beyond that which is expected by the end of the EYFS.

Formative assessment
Ongoing observation and assessment of children in order to make professional judgements about children's achievements and decide on the next steps in learning.

Internal moderation
Practitioners' agreement of assessment judgements with others within their own settings.

Level descriptor
Outlines the knowledge, skills and understanding required for each level of attainment in each subject of the national curriculum.

Measuring progress
Involves comparing assessments of a child's attainment at different points in time to determine whether that child has made gains in learning and development.

Moderation
The discussion based on a representative sample of judgements between moderators and practitioners which establishes:

- the consistency and accuracy of judgements made by different practitioners;
- whether the judgements about children's learning and development are in line with the nationally agreed exemplification; and
- whether the process of assessment provides for reliable, accurate and secure data.

Observation
Reaching an understanding of children's learning by watching, listening to, and interacting with children as they engage in activities and experiences and demonstrate their specific knowledge, skills and understanding.

Parents
The term 'parent' is used to refer to:

- parents of a child;
- any person who is not a parent of a child but who has parental responsibility for the child; and
- any person who has care of the child.

Playing and exploring
Refers to engagement comprising three aspects:

- finding out and exploring;
- using what children know in their play; and
- being willing to have a go.

Practitioner
Any adult who works with children in a setting.

Practitioner knowledge

Refers to the understanding reached about a child's attainment through observation of everyday activities and experiences. It is underpinned by specific examples and demonstrations of a child's attainment which may not be formally recorded.

Reception class

An entry class to primary school for children who have their fifth birthday during the school year and, where it is appropriate, including children who are younger or older than five. Defined by Section 142 of the School Standards and Framework Act 1998.

Responsible pedagogy

Enables each child to demonstrate learning in the fullest sense. It depends on the use of assessment information to plan relevant and motivating learning experiences for each child. Effective assessment can only take place when children have the opportunity to demonstrate their understanding, learning and development in a range of contexts.

Setting

Any out-of-home provider of Early Years provision for children from birth to five, such as childminders, LA nurseries, nursery or Early Years centres, children's centres, playgroups, pre-schools, or schools in the independent, private or voluntary sector and maintained schools.

Stakeholder

A person or organisation that has an interest in the EYFS Profile assessments. The key stakeholders are parents and children. They also include staff in the setting, LA and the Department who uses the information for a range of purposes.

Annex 1: EYFS Profile

Name..........................   Age in months..........................

Characteristics of effective learning	How (name of child) learns
By playing and exploring: • finding out and exploring • using what they know in their play • being willing to have a go	
Through active learning: • being involved and concentrating • keeping on trying • enjoying achieving what they set out to do	
By creating and thinking critically • having their own ideas • using what they already know to learn new things • choosing ways to do things and finding new ways	

Area of learning		Aspect	Emerging	Expected	Exceeding
Communication and language	ELG 01	Listening and attention			
	ELG 02	Understanding			
	ELG 03	Speaking			
Physical development	ELG 04	Moving and handling			
	ELG 05	Health and self-care			
Personal, social and emotional development	ELG 06	Self-confidence and self-awareness			
	ELG 07	Managing feelings and behaviour			
	ELG 08	Making relationships			
Literacy	ELG 09	Reading			
	ELG 10	Writing			
Mathematics	ELG 11	Numbers			
	ELG 12	Shapes, space and measures			
Understanding the world	ELG 13	People and communities			
	ELG 14	The world			
	ELG 15	Technology			
Expressive arts and design	ELG 16	Exploring and using media and materials			
	ELG 17	Being imaginative			

Annex 2: Additional information for the 'exceeding' judgement

The descriptors detailed below are sourced from the Tickell Review. They act as guidance to support the process of making a judgement that a child's level of learning and development is in the 'exceeding' category. Please refer to section 2.3 for further information.

The areas of learning of EYFS and their associated 'exceeding' descriptors

	Prime areas of learning	
	Communication and language	
01	**Listening and attention:** Children listen to instructions and follow them accurately, asking for clarification if necessary. They listen attentively with sustained concentration to follow a story without pictures or props and can listen in a larger group, for example, at assembly.	
02	**Understanding:** After listening to stories children can express views about events or characters in the story and answer questions about why things happened. They can carry out instructions which contain several parts in a sequence.	
03	**Speaking:** Children show some awareness of the listener by making changes to language and non-verbal features. They recount experiences and imagine possibilities, often connecting ideas. They use a range of vocabulary in imaginative ways to add information, express ideas or to explain or justify actions or events.	
	Physical development	
04	**Moving and handling:** Children can hop confidently and skip in time to music. They hold paper in position and use their preferred hand for writing, using a correct pencil grip. They are beginning to be able to write on lines and control letter size.	
05	**Health and self-care:** Children know about and can make healthy choices in relation to healthy eating and exercise. They can dress and undress independently, successfully managing fastening buttons or laces.	
	Personal, social and emotional development	
06	**Self-confidence and self-awareness:** Children are confident to speak to a class group. They can talk about the things they enjoy, and are good at, and about the things they do not find easy. They are resourceful in finding support when they need help or information. They can talk about the plans they have made to carry out activities and what they might change if they were to repeat them.	
07	**Managing feelings and behaviour:** Children know some ways to manage their feelings and are beginning to use these to maintain control. They can listen to each other's suggestions and plan how to achieve an outcome without adult help. They know when and how to stand up for themselves appropriately. They can stop and think before acting and they can wait for things they want.	
08	**Making relationships:** Children play group games with rules. They understand someone else's point of view can be different from theirs. They resolve minor disagreements through listening to each other to come up with a fair solution. They understand what bullying is and that this is unacceptable behaviour.	

	Specific areas of learning
	Literacy
09	**Reading:** Children can read phonically regular words of more than one syllable as well as many irregular but high frequency words. They use phonic, semantic and syntactic knowledge to understand unfamiliar vocabulary. They can describe the main events in the simple stories they have read.
10	**Writing:** Children can spell phonically regular words of more than one syllable as well as many irregular but high frequency words. They use key features of narrative in their own writing.
	Mathematics
11	**Numbers:** Children estimate a number of objects and check quantities by counting up to 20. They solve practical problems that involve combining groups of 2, 5 or 10, or sharing into equal groups. (This descriptor has been amended to reflect the increased level of challenge applied to the expected descriptor following the Tickell review.)
12	**Shape, space and measures:** Children estimate, measure, weigh and compare and order objects and talk about properties, position and time.
	Understanding the world
13	**People and communities:** Children know the difference between past and present events in their own lives and some reasons why people's lives were different in the past. They know that other children have different likes and dislikes and that they may be good at different things. They understand that different people have different beliefs, attitudes, customs and traditions and why it is important to treat them with respect.
14	**The world:** Children know that the environment and living things are influenced by human activity. They can describe some actions which people in their own community do that help to maintain the area they live in. They know the properties of some materials and can suggest some of the purposes they are used for. They are familiar with basic scientific concepts such as floating, sinking,experimentation.
15	**Technology:** Children find out about and use a range of everyday technology. They select appropriate applications that support an identified need – for example in deciding how best to make a record of a special event in their lives, such as a journey on a steam train.
	Expressive arts and design
16	**Exploring and using media and materials:** Children develop their own ideas through selecting and using materials and working on processes that interest them. Through their explorations they find out and make decisions about how media and materials can be combined and changed.
17	**Being imaginative:** Children talk about the ideas and processes which have led them to make music, designs, images or products. They can talk about features of their own and others work, recognising the differences between them and the strengths of others.

Annex 3: Examples of lines of enquiry to be followed when completing the commentary for each characteristic of effective learning

Playing and exploring – engagement

Finding out and exploring is concerned with the child's open-ended hands-on experiences which result from innate curiosity and provide the raw sensory material from which the child builds concepts, tests ideas and finds out.

Possible lines of enquiry:

- Does the child respond to first hand experiences in an exploratory way?
- How does the child demonstrate natural curiosity?
- Does the child notice patterns, changes, similarities and differences when exploring across the curriculum?

Using what they know in their play describes how children use play to bring together their current understandings, combining, refining and exploring their ideas in imaginative ways. Representing experiences through imaginative play supports the development of narrative thought, the ability to see from other perspectives, and symbolic thinking.

Possible lines of enquiry:

- In what ways does the child use what he or she discovers in play and link it to existing knowledge?
- Can the child combine, refine and explore ideas in imaginative ways?
- Can the child see things from other perspectives?

Being willing to have a go refers to the child finding an interest, initiating activities, seeking challenge, having a 'can do' orientation, being willing to take a risk in new experiences, and developing the view of failures as opportunities to learn.

Possible lines of enquiry:

- Does the child initiate activities around own interests?
- Does the child seek challenges and take risks in new experiences?
- Does the child learn from mistakes without becoming disheartened?

Active learning - motivation

Being involved and concentrating describes the intensity of attention that arises from children concentrating on following a line of interest in their activities.

Possible lines of enquiry:

- To what extent does the child become completely focussed in activities and experiences and not easily distracted?
- To what extent does the child show intensity of attention for example by being concerned about details in activities, experiences and ideas?

Keeping on trying refers to the importance of persistence even in the face of challenge or difficulties, an element of purposeful control which supports resilience

Possible lines of enquiry:

- Does the child pursue a particular line of interest in an activity?
- Does the child demonstrate persistence in the face of difficulty or a challenge?
- Can the child refocus and re-plan to overcome difficulties, setbacks and disappointments?
- Does the child know how to seek appropriate help in terms of materials, tools and other people?

Enjoying achieving what they set out to do refers to the reward of meeting one's own goals, building on the intrinsic motivation which supports long-term success, rather than relying on the approval of others.

Possible lines of enquiry:

- Does the child become involved in activities and experiences which arise out of personal interest, curiosity and enquiry?
- Does the child demonstrate satisfaction when engaged in and completing personal endeavours?

Creating and thinking critically

Having their own ideas covers the critical area of creativity – generating new ideas and approaches in all areas of endeavour. Being inventive allows children to find new problems as they seek challenges, and to explore ways of solving these.

Possible lines of enquiry:

- Does the child generate new ideas during activities?
- Does the child adapt, refine or make changes when previous ideas were unsuccessful or could be developed?
- Is the child inventive in solving problems, using and synthesising knowledge and skills across areas of learning?

Using what they know to learn new things refers to the way in which children develop and link concepts, find meaning in sequence, cause and effect and in the intentions of others through both narrative and scientific modes of thought.

Possible lines of enquiry:

- Does the child talk about or explore the idea of cause and effect through actions?
- Does the child use acquired knowledge and skills to explore new learning across and within areas of learning?
- Does the child offer ideas of why things happen and how things work or show this in exploratory play?

Choosing ways to do things and finding new ways involves approaching goal-directed activity in organised ways, making choices and decisions about how to approach tasks, planning and monitoring what to do and being able to change strategies.

Possible lines of enquiry:

- Does the child explore ways of solving new problems including trial and error?
- Is the child able to plan and monitor what has been done?
- Can the child change strategies when appropriate?

Annex 4: Role specification

Post-holders need to demonstrate the following knowledge, skills and experience in order to successfully perform the moderator's role:

- professional discussion with the practitioner on a moderation visit;
- the ability to establish and validate the accuracy of practitioner judgements in line with national exemplification materials;
- effective verbal and written feedback to practitioners including recommendations for further training, if appropriate; and
- an understanding of the EYFS Profile moderation process.

Knowledge and experience	
B.Ed., Cert. Education or other degree and PGCE	E
Knowledge and experience	
Current knowledge of EYFS and recent experience of teaching in an Early Years setting	E
Current knowledge of the principles and purpose of the EYFS Profile	E
Understanding of national exemplification materials	E
Knowledge of EYFS Profile moderation process	E
Experience of management and implementation of the EYFS Profile moderation	D
Evidence of further professional development (eg as advanced skills teacher or lead teacher)	D
Experience of working with children with special educational needs or for whom English is not their home language	D
Capabilities and skills	
To communicate effectively and be receptive to new information	E
To question and challenge practitioner judgements appropriately	E
To scrutinise, distil and interpret evidence and make decisions confidently	E
To provide feedback and remain objective in a range of circumstances	E
To build professional relationships with individuals and groups	E

Annex 5: Blank exemplar moderation visit note

Name of school or setting	
Headteacher/manager	

Term/Year		Date of visit		Duration of visit	
Moderator name					
Practitioner names: NQT/new to Reception?/ years in Reception?			Experience		
			Experience		

Please indicate below which ELG and level of development were moderated for each of the sampled profiles. Where practitioner judgements could not be validated for any ELG, please annotate the form and record the detail in the outcomes box.

Area of learning	ELG		Profile 1	Profile 2	Profile 3	Profile 4	Profile 5
Communication and language	ELG 01	Listening and attention					
	ELG 02	Understanding					
	ELG 03	Speaking					
Physical development	ELG 04	Moving and handling					
	ELG 05	Health and self-care					
Personal, social and emotional development	ELG 06	Self-confidence and self-awareness					
	ELG 07	Managing feelings and behaviour					
	ELG 08	Making relationships					
Literacy	ELG 09	Reading					
	ELG 10	Writing					

Area of learning	ELG		Profile 1	Profile 2	Profile 3	Profile 4	Profile 5
Mathematics	ELG 11	Numbers					
	ELG 12	Shapes, space and measures					
Understanding the world	ELG 13	People and communities					
	ELG 14	The world					
	ELG 15	Technology					
Expressive arts and design	ELG 16	Exploring and using media and materials					
	ELG 17	Being imaginative					

EYFS Profile judgements	
Are judgements consistent and accurate? Is the evidence supporting the children's attainment appropriate? How does the evidence match the band descriptor? Have you observed consistent and independent behaviour? Is the child initiated/adult directed ratio appropriate? Does the description of the child's characteristics of effective learning match the child's overall attainment?	
Contributors to the process	
Who contributes to the children's profiles within the school/setting? How are the parents' contributions valued and included within their child's profile assessments? How are the children's contributions represented in the profiles?	
Strengths	
Do practitioners' have a thorough knowledge of the children? Did internal moderation/linking with other settings take place?	

Agreed action points

	Outcome
Practitioner judgements are **ACCURATE**; in line with exemplification	☐
Practitioner judgements are **NOT ACCURATE**; in line with exemplification	☐

Detail:

Signatures	Headteacher	
	Moderator	
	Practitioner	
	Practitioner	

Setting comments on the moderation visit	LA moderation manager details

EYFS

2014

National curriculum assessments

Assessment and reporting arrangements

Early years foundation stage

About this publication

Who is it for?

Local authorities, headteachers, governing bodies and all early years education providers and education professionals with responsibility for assessing, reporting or moderating the EYFS profile.

What does it cover?

- Information and guidance on EYFS profile assessments and administration.

- Information about moderation of the EYFS profile.

Related information

Visit the Department for Education's website at www.education.gov.uk/eyfs for all related information.

For more copies

Printed copies like this one can be purchased from www.thenationalcurriculum.com. Electronic versions of this material can also be downloaded from the DfE's website at www.education.gov.uk/eyfs.

The 'Assessment and reporting arrangements' (ARA) contains provisions made pursuant to Articles 3 and 4 of the EYFS (Learning and Development Requirements) Order 2007 (S.I. 2007/1772) (amended in 2012). This Order is made under sections 39(1)(a), 42 and 44 of the Childcare Act 2006.

The ARA gives full effect to, or otherwise supplements the provisions made in the Order, and as such has effect as if made by the Order. The ARA provides information and guidance on the early years foundation stage profile and its administration.

Please discard and recycle previous printed versions of this guidance.

1. Introduction

1.1 What is the ARA?

The 'Assessment and reporting arrangements' (ARA) contains details on assessing and reporting the Early years foundation stage (EYFS) profile in 2013 to 2014.

This document is produced by the Standards and Testing Agency (STA), an executive agency of the Department for Education (DfE). It is responsible for developing and delivering all statutory assessments from early years to the end of key stage 3, and will ensure that EYFS profile outcomes are reliable as a result of robust moderation practice.

STA's framework document, which gives more detail on its operation, is available from the DfE's website at www.education.gov.uk/sta.

The term 'parent' is used in this document as defined in section 576 of the Education Act 1996 as:

- parents of a child;
- any person who is not a parent of a child but who has parental responsibility for the child; and
- any person who has care of the child.

All references to academies include free schools, as in law they are academies.

All references to EYFS settings include any out-of-home provider of early years provision for children from birth to five, such as childminders, local authority nurseries, nursery or early years centres, children's centres, playgroups, pre-schools, or schools in the independent, private or voluntary sector and maintained schools.

All information, including dates, is correct at the time of printing and subject to change. Any changes will be communicated to headteachers, managers and local authorities.

1.2 Legal status of the ARA

The EYFS is a comprehensive statutory framework published in 2012 by the DfE. The framework sets standards for development, learning and care of children from birth to the age of five.

Section 40(2)(a) of the Childcare Act 2006 stipulates that early years providers must ensure that their provision meets the learning and development requirements as specified in the EYFS (Learning and Development Requirements) Order 2007 (S.I. 2007/1772) (amended in 2012). The Act states that this Order can specify the arrangements which are required for assessing children for the purpose of ascertaining what they have achieved in relation to the early learning goals (ELGs).

All English local authorities must have regard to any guidance given by STA in exercising their function under the EYFS (Learning and Development Requirements) Order 2007, article 4.2. The learning and development requirements are given legal force by an Order made under section 39 (1)(a), 42 and 44 of the Childcare Act 2006.

This ARA provides further guidance on the EYFS profile, which is set out in the statutory framework for the EYFS, available on the DfE's website at www.education.gov.uk/eyfs.

1.3 How does this ARA apply to different EYFS settings?

The ARA applies to all early years settings, including maintained schools, non-maintained schools, independent schools and all providers on the early years register.

Academies in England

Academies must implement the requirements of the EYFS as set out in section 40 of the Childcare Act 2006 and comply with local authority moderation requirements.

All registered early years providers are required to complete the EYFS assessment for any children in the final year of the EYFS and to participate in moderation. This includes an academy providing for children in the final year of the EYFS.

Funding for EYFS moderation activities for all schools rests within local authority budgets.

Details of funding agreements for all academies are available on the DfE's website at www.education.gov.uk/aboutdfe/executiveagencies/efa/b00213953/academies-funding-2013-14 .

Overseas schools

Service children's education (SCE) schools are required to participate in early years national curriculum assessment and reporting arrangements in line with the arrangements for administration in England.

All other overseas schools cannot participate formally, but may choose to download the 'Early years foundation stage profile handbook' from the DfE's website at www.education.gov.uk/eyfsp.

Pupil referral units, hospital schools and children educated at home

Children attending a pupil referral unit (PRU) or hospital school are not subject to the assessment requirements in this ARA. Children still on the register at a maintained school but attending a PRU or hospital school are required to be assessed, and the results should be reported by the home school.

These assessment and reporting arrangements do not apply to children who are being educated at home, unless they are on the register of a maintained school or independent school.

Independent schools and EYFS providers registered with Ofsted under the Childcare Act 2006

All independent schools and registered EYFS providers must comply with the information in this document unless they have an exemption from the EYFS learning and development requirements[1]. This includes participating in moderation arrangements for the EYFS profile and submission of EYFS profile data to the local authority (this data collection is governed by section 99 of the Childcare Act 2006), as specified in the table in section 2.2.1.

All settings with children who are not in receipt of government funding

Under section 99 of the Childcare Act 2006, local authorities are allowed to collect EYFS profile data with contextual child data for children not in receipt of government funding in the summer term. EYFS providers are required to comply with local authority requests for this data. Local authorities are not required to submit this data to the DfE.

The local authority can request data including:

- the learning and development category for each ELG
- the child's date of birth
- the home address where the child normally resides
- the child's ethnic group
- the child's gender
- whether the child has a special educational need
- if the child has English as an additional language (EAL)

1.4 Responsibilities

All those responsible for assessing and reporting on the EYFS need to refer to this document and ensure they are aware of any changes from previous years.

The ARA provides guidance on the responsibilities of those involved in assessment and reporting for the EYFS. EYFS profile assessments must be completed for all children in the final year of the EYFS who will be five years old on or before Sunday 31 August 2014, although some exceptions apply (see section 2.1).

The EYFS profile must be completed no later than Friday 4 July 2014. This date applies to all EYFS providers, including maintained schools, non-maintained schools, independent schools, children's centres, academies and childcare providers registered by Ofsted on the early years register. The EYFS profile must be completed by the provider at the setting where the child spends the majority of their time between 8am and 6pm.

---

1   Independent schools registered with the DfE that are not academies can take up an exemption from the learning and development requirements if they meet the conditions set out in the Direction from the Secretary of State – details are available from the DfE website www.education.gov.uk/eyfs in the document 'Guidance on exemptions for Early Years providers'.

Headteachers

All headteachers and managers of EYFS provision have a duty to implement the EYFS. They must ensure their schools and settings comply with the learning and development requirements of the EYFS, including completing the EYFS profile and involvement in local authority moderation activities.

Headteachers must:

- ensure an EYFS profile is completed for all eligible children and data is quality assured;

- ensure provision is made to meet the requirements of all children with special educational needs (SEN);

- take responsibility for the reliability of their EYFS profile outcomes and ensure that the data accurately reflects the level of attainment of the current cohort of children;

- ensure teacher judgements are monitored;

- ensure EYFS profile data is returned to the local authority in accordance with the table in section 2.2.1;

- provide EYFS profile assessments to their school's governing body to enable it to comply with national data submission requirements and report to parents;

- provide parents with a written report of the child's progress against the EYFS ELGs and the opportunity for discussion;

- where a parent requests it, provide a copy of the EYFS profile report on their child's progress, free of charge; and

- ensure the statutory requirements for the transfer of records between providers are fulfilled, including the completion of the common transfer file.

Local authorities

Local authorities must:

- ensure that schools and other EYFS providers understand and follow the requirements set out in the ARA;

- provide schools and other EYFS providers with training (including agreement trialling[2]);

- provide advice on all aspects of assessment at EYFS;

- ensure the accuracy and consistency of the assessments made by early years providers in their geographical area by ensuring moderation of the EYFS profile is carried out in all schools, academies and other settings, as specified in the ARA and section 6.4 of the 'EYFS profile handbook';

- ensure schools have a secure electronic system to submit EYFS profile data;

---

2   Agreement trialling is the process of discussing assessment judgements in a group in order to ensure that all practitioners understand the national exemplification of standards and apply them consistently.

- ensure all other EYFS providers have appropriate means by which to accurately record EYFS profile results and submit data to their local authority if requested (see the table in section 2.2.1 for EYFS profile data submission requirements);

- collect EYFS profile data, and quality assure and submit it to the DfE in the required format by the due dates (see the table in section 2.2.1 for EYFS profile data submission requirements); and

- inform STA without delay of any irregularities in their assessment arrangements.

1.5 Concerns and complaints

Concerns and complaints should be raised with STA by writing to the Stakeholder relations team at STA, 53–55 Butts Road, Earlsdon Park, Coventry, CV1 3BH, or by emailing assessments@education.gov.uk.

Where EYFS settings feel that their concerns have not been fully addressed by STA in line with the published procedures, regulatory concerns can be raised with the Office of Qualifications and Examinations Regulation (Ofqual). Enquiries and concerns can be sent to Ofqual at Spring Place, Coventry Business Park, Herald Avenue, Coventry CV5 6UB, or by emailing info@ofqual.gov.uk.

2. The early years foundation stage profile

The 2014 'EYFS profile handbook' contains detailed information on the background and purpose of the EYFS profile, as well as how the profile should be completed. The 'EYFS profile handbook' is available on the DfE's website at www.education.gov.uk/eyfsp.

Headteachers should make sure all those involved in assessment of the EYFS have a thorough understanding of the 'EYFS profile handbook'.

2.1 Completing the EYFS profile

The EYFS profile must be completed for each child who will be five years old on or before Sunday 31 August 2014 unless:

- an exemption from the profile has been granted for the setting by the Secretary of State;

- the child is continuing in EYFS provision beyond the year in which they turn five;

- the child has arrived from abroad less than two weeks before the profile submission deadline and so an accurate and valid assessment cannot be completed; or

- the child has spent the majority of the academic year away from the setting, for example, due to illness or medical treatment.

Profile judgements should be made on the basis of cumulative observational evidence recorded over the course of the year. Profile summaries must be completed no later than Friday 4 July 2014.

2.2 Data collection and submission

EYFS providers may use any secure system to collect and submit EYFS data, as long as it enables practitioners to record completed profile data for every child at the end of the EYFS. However, EYFS providers should agree the preferred system with their local authority.

For providers without a suitable electronic system, a collection spreadsheet for 2014 will be available from the DfE's website.

The spreadsheet can be used to enter EYFS profile assessment scale summary scores and create a CSV export file for up 150 children's EYFS profile results.

The spreadsheet, along with more information and guidance on data collection and submission is available on the DfE's website at www.education.gov.uk/researchandstatistics/stats/eyfs.

2.2.1 National data submission

The following table sets out the requirements for submission of EYFS profile data and contextual child data to local authorities and the DfE.

Status of child and setting	Is submission of data to local authority statutory?	Is local authority submission to DfE statutory?
Child in a maintained school	✓	✓
Child in EYFS provision, who is in receipt of government funding in the 2014 summer term	✓	✓
Child in EYFS provision, who is not in receipt of government funding in the 2014 summer term	✓ Where requested by local authority	✗
Child in an academy	✓	✓
Child in an independent school which is in receipt of government funding in the 2014 summer term	✓	✓
Child in an independent school which is not in receipt of government funding in the 2014 summer term	✓ Where requested by local authority	✗
Child with a registered childminder (for the majority of the time they spend within EYFS provision between 8am and 6pm)	✓ Where required by local authority - or if the child is in receipt of government funding in the 2014 summer term	✗ Unless child in receipt of government funding in the 2014 summer term
Child in an independent EYFS provision where the setting has EYFS exemption	✓ On a voluntary basis	✗
Child being educated at home	✗ Unless on the register of a maintained/ independent school	✗ Unless on the register of a maintained/ independent school

The child's name is not required from settings which are not in receipt of government funding. The local authority is only required to submit data to the DfE for children who receive government funding in the 2014 summer term.

If a child transfers schools then the schools involved should agree which school will submit the data. This will usually be the school where the child is registered at the point when data is submitted.

The DfE will send full details of the data submission arrangements to local authorities in early 2014. Although it is not a statutory requirement, settings and local authorities are encouraged to return data to the DfE on a voluntary basis to help produce a full picture of children's attainment.

2.2.2 Data specification

Assessment rating	EYFS judgement
1	Indicates a child who is at the 'emerging' level at the end of the EYFS
2	Indicates a child who is at the 'expected' level at the end of the EYFS
3	Indicates a child who is at the 'exceeding' level at the end of the EYFS
A	Indicates a child who has not been assessed due to long periods of absence, for instance a prolonged illness or arrives too late in the summer term for teacher assessment to be carried out, or for an exemption

2.3 Exceptions

2.3.1 Exemptions from the assessment arrangements

All EYFS settings must participate in the assessment arrangements outlined in this ARA, unless they have been granted an exemption by the Secretary of State. If an individual child is granted an exemption from the assessment arrangements then this should be recorded as 'A' for each ELG in their profile return.

More information about EYFS profile exemptions is available on the DfE's website at www.education.gov.uk/eyfs.

2.3.2 Alternative assessments

The EYFS profile is an inclusive assessment, capable of capturing a wide range of children's learning and development outcomes. The observation and assessment of some children might be particularly challenging for practitioners. If an outcome of 'emerging' is given, it might not provide the full picture about that child's learning and development at the end of the EYFS.

In these cases, additional information should be considered alongside EYFS profile judgements to ensure that conversations between EYFS and key stage 1 staff are meaningful and lead to the child's successful transition.

There may be cases where it is not appropriate to make a judgement against an assessment scale, for instance if the child has recently arrived from abroad. In these cases, practitioners must use 'A' (for no assessment) when the data is submitted to the local authority.

2.3.3 Children who remain in EYFS provision beyond the age of five

The expectation is that children will move with their peers and will therefore be assessed only once for the EYFS profile. In exceptional circumstances, after discussion and in agreement with parents, a child might remain in EYFS provision beyond the end of the academic year in which he or she reaches the age of five. Care should be taken that this decision does not prejudice the child's personal, social and emotional development.

In these exceptional cases, assessment should continue throughout the child's time within EYFS provision and an EYFS profile should be completed at the end of the year before the child moves on to the key stage 1 programme of study. The setting should discuss its intention to defer the child's statutory assessment with the local authority EYFS profile moderation manager. This will ensure the child's data is not considered missing when the setting submits EYFS profile outcomes for the current cohort.

Care must be taken when entering the child's EYFS profile assessment into any electronic recording system as the date of birth may now be outside the expected range for the cohort. Local authorities should provide instructions to settings in such cases. The DfE will consider the child to be part of this new cohort, and will accept data submitted in this way, although a check may be made with the local authority as to the accuracy of the dates of birth of individual children.

3. Moderating the EYFS profile

3.1 Internal moderation

The moderation of EYFS profile assessments begins within each individual setting. It is supported by local authorities, or local authority approved agencies, through a programme of visits and meetings. Within their own settings, practitioners can agree assessment judgements with others informally. This might involve two practitioners, for example a teacher and a teaching assistant or a reception class teacher and a year 1 teacher, discussing evidence about a child's development.

3.2 Local authority requirements for moderation

Local authorities have a statutory responsibility to set up and implement moderation arrangements in order to:

- secure the consistency and accuracy of judgements made by different practitioners;

- reassure practitioners that their judgements are accurate, valid and consistent with national standards; and

- assure moderators that an acceptable level of accuracy and validity has been achieved for assessments recorded and reported by the settings for which they have responsibility.

Moderation of the EYFS profile is a sampling process and not a method for checking each child's attainment. Local authority moderation visits use professional discussions to check teachers' ability to make accurate assessments and apply them consistently. Evidence discussed includes materials, knowledge of the child, anecdotal incidents, results of observations or information from additional sources that supports the overall picture of a child's development. There is no requirement that evidence should be formally recorded or documented and the extent to which the practitioner chooses to record information will depend on individual preference. Paperwork should be kept to the minimum that practitioners require to illustrate, support and recall their knowledge of the child's attainment. The outcome of moderation should be recorded.

The 2014 'EYFS profile handbook' provides local authorities with guidelines and examples of effective moderation practice. Local authorities must ensure[3] that:

- 25 per cent of settings receive a moderation visit annually, which scrutinises all 17 ELGs.

- The remaining 75 per cent of settings attend EYFS profile training (including agreement trialling activities) annually.

- Training in EYFS assessment and the completion of the EYFS profile summaries is offered to all providers who require it.

---

3   Section 13 of the Childcare Act 2006 requires local authorities to secure the provision of information, advice and training, for childcare providers, prospective providers and childcare employees.

- EYFS profile assessment judgements are moderated. They appoint and train moderators with appropriate experience of the EYFS and the ELGs to secure consistent standards in assessment judgements.

- All providers are visited regularly as part of a cycle of moderation visits, and providers are notified of whether the EYFS profile assessment is being carried out in accordance with requirements.

- Settings that are to receive an EYFS profile moderation visit are informed of this by the end of the spring term. For moderation purposes, these settings will need to complete interim judgements against all ELGs at the beginning of May for children in the final year of the EYFS.

If the local authority moderator judges the assessment is not in line with the exemplified standards, the local authority can require the provider to arrange for the practitioner to participate in further training/moderation activities, and to reconsider their assessments as advised by the moderator.

All English local authorities must have regard to any guidance produced by STA in exercising their function under the EYFS (Learning and Development Requirements) Order 2007, Article 4(2). This means that the local authority should exercise the powers and duties in the way the guidance sets out. Where a local authority chooses to undertake a moderation model not reliant on moderation visits, the local authority must ensure it can demonstrate that all the key elements of the moderation visit are protected. Any deviation which does not have regard to STA guidance would be deemed as not meeting statutory requirements.

3.3 Headteachers, governing bodies and managers of early years settings

Headteachers, governing bodies and managers of early years settings must:

- arrange for practitioners responsible for the completion of EYFS profiles to take part in local authority moderation activities at least once a year;

- allow the local authority moderator to enter the premises at all reasonable times to carry out moderation visits;

- meet reasonable requests from the moderator to amend assessments and for practitioners to take part in further training/moderation activities;

- take responsibility for the reliability of their EYFS profile outcomes using quality assurance processes and ensure that the data accurately reflects the attainment of the current cohort of children;

- permit the relevant local authority to examine and take copies of documents and other articles relating to the EYFS profile and assessments; and

- provide the relevant local authority with such information relating to the EYFS profile and assessment as it may reasonably request.

They also have a general responsibility to ensure that the practitioners involved in making the assessments have the opportunity to become familiar with effective practice. This may involve:

- attendance at training courses;
- visits by moderators to settings;
- moderation meetings within settings (in-house moderation); and
- moderation meetings with practitioners from other settings.

4. Reporting and using results

4.1 Reporting assessment of children's development to parents

All EYFS providers must give parents a written summary of a child's attainment against the ELGs.

Parents should be involved in the assessment process on a regular, ongoing basis and be encouraged to participate in their child's learning and development.

For children at the end of reception year, providers should report:

- whether children are meeting expected levels of development, or if they are exceeding expected levels, or not yet reaching expected levels ('emerging') for each ELG;
- brief particulars of attainment in all areas of learning;
- comments on general progress including the characteristics of effective learning; and
- arrangements for discussing the report.

At the end of reception year, parents should receive a written summary reporting attainment against the ELGs. Practitioners may use the information provided by EYFS profile assessment as a basis for their reports to parents. Reports should be specific to the child, concise, informative and help to identify appropriate next steps.

Settings must offer parents a reasonable opportunity to discuss the outcomes of the EYFS profile with their child's teacher. This meeting should be within the term in which the EYFS profile has been completed. Teachers may wish to consider making the child's profile available to parents as part of this discussion. If parents ask to see a copy of their child's

profile, the setting must make this available.

4.2 Children who transfer to a new school

Schools are required[4] to transfer a child's educational record and common transfer file to any new school to which a child transfers in England, Wales, Scotland and Northern Ireland. The means of transfer to a school outside England must be in line with the arrangements for transfer between schools in England. In addition:

If a child transfers schools then the schools involved should agree which school will submit the child's results to the local authority. This will usually be the school where the child is registered at the point when data is submitted.

---

4   The Education (Pupil Information) (England) Regulations 2005 (S.I. 2005/1437) (and subsequent amendments set out in the Education (Pupil information) (England) (Amendment) Regulations 2008 (S.I. 2008/1747)). See: www.legislation.gov.uk/uksi/2008/1747/contents/made.

Copies of every report forming part of a child's educational record must also be transferred automatically when a child changes school. Certain information, including teacher assessment, is transferred securely via the common transfer file.

Governing body responsibilities

The governing body must arrange to have the following information sent to the child's new school:

- the child's educational record; and
- the defined items of data that comprise the common transfer file.

Further information on the common transfer file is available on the DfE's website at www.education.gov.uk/researchandstatistics/datatdatam/ctf.

This task is commonly delegated to headteachers by governing bodies. The information must be sent within 15 school days of the child ceasing to be registered at the old school, unless the new school is not known. In this case it should be sent within 15 school days of any request from the child's new school.

Where a child's school is not established within a reasonable time, schools should follow guidance on the DfE's website at www.education.gov.uk/schools/adminandfinance and send the common transfer file to a special area for secure file transfer on the DfE's website that forms a database of 'missing' children. Similarly, schools that do not receive common transfer files for new children can ask their local authority to search the database for the files.

How should the information be sent to the new school?

Where both the old and the new school have the necessary facilities, the common transfer file must be sent to the new school either:

- through the secure file transfer service on the DfE's website at www.education.gov.uk/schools/adminandfinance; or
- over a secure network that can only be accessed by the local authority, the governing body or a teacher at any school within that local authority.

The basic requirement is that the old school will send the educational records and common transfer file to the new school by one of these methods. However, if either school does not have the facilities to send or receive information in this format, then local authorities may provide the file where there are agreed and secure local arrangements to that effect.

What information should be included in the common transfer file?

The statutory information that should automatically form part of the common transfer file is outlined on the DfE's website at www.education.gov.uk/researchandstatistics/datatdatam/ctf.

Management information system suppliers will usually provide further guidance to schools, specific to their system.

4.3 How EYFS profile assessment results are used

EYFS profile assessment data is used to inform year 1 teachers about each child's development and learning needs. Providers should ensure that year 1 teachers receive all the information detailed in section 4.2. It can also be a source of information about levels of development within a school or setting. For example:

- levels of learning and development in each of the areas of learning for individual children, classes and year groups;
- the attainment of children born in different months of the year; and
- the attainment of different groups of children, for example boys and girls.

Schools may also wish to conduct further analysis using wider contextual information.

National and local authority data will be published on the DfE's website so that schools can compare their children's attainment on a regional and national basis.

There are no achievement and attainment tables for the EYFS.

5. Contact details

Please make sure you have your seven-digit Department for Education number before you call, for example 123/4567.

National curriculum assessments helpline For general enquiries about national curriculum tests	**Tel:** 0300 303 3013 **Email:** assessments@education.gov.uk **Website:** www.education.gov.uk/assessment
STA distribution helpline For enquiries about deliveries of standard and modified test materials	**Tel:** 0800 169 4195
STA modified test helpline For guidance on ordering modified test materials	**Tel:** 0300 303 3019 **Email:** schooltests@rnib.org.uk
STA orderline To access previous years' national curriculum test materials	**Tel:** 0300 303 3015 **Website:** http://orderline.education.gov.uk (available until Monday 30 June 2014)
Department for Education national enquiry line For enquiries about the statutory requirements for assessment, national results, performance tables and reporting to parents	**Tel:** 0370 000 2288 **Website:** www.education.gov.uk/contactus
EduBase To keep your school's contact details up to date	**Website:** www.education.gov.uk/edubase
Information Commissioner's Office For enquiries about the Data Protection Act 1998	**Tel:** 0303 123 1113 **Website:** www.ico.gov.uk
Ofqual For regulatory concerns	**Tel:** 0300 303 3346 **Email:** info@ofqual.gov.uk **Website:** www.ofqual.gov.uk